T0145596

Maximize Your Potential Through the Power of Your Subconscious Mind to Overcome Fear and Worry

Series Titles

Maximize Your Potential Through the Power of Your Subconscious Mind for a More Spiritual Life

Maximize Your Potential Through the Power of Your Subconscious Mind for an Enriched Life

Maximize Your Potential Through the Power of Your Subconscious Mind for Health and Vitality

Maximize Your Potential Through the Power of Your Subconscious Mind to Create Wealth and Success

Maximize Your Potential Through the Power of Your Subconscious Mind to Develop Self Confidence and Self Esteem

Maximize Your Potential Through the Power of Your Subconscious Mind to Overcome Fear and Worry

Maximize Your Potential Through the Power of Your Subconscious Mind to Overcome Fear and Worry

One of a Series of Six New Books

Joseph Murphy, DD, Ph.D.

Edited and Updated for the 21st Century
by Arthur R. Pell, Ph.D.

Published 2019 by Gildan Media LLC
aka G&D Media
www.GandDmedia.com

MAXIMIZE YOUR POTENTIAL THROUGH THE POWER OF YOUR SUBCONSCIOUS
MIND TO OVERCOME FEAR AND WORRY. Copyright © Joseph Murphy Trust. All
rights exclusively licensed by JMW Group Inc., jmwgroup@jmwgroup.net.

Front cover design by David Rheinhardt of Pyrographx

Interior design by Meghan Day Healey of Story Horse, LLC

Library of Congress Cataloging-in-Publication Data is available upon request

ISBN: 978-1-7225-0260-7

10   9   8   7   6   5   4   3   2   1

CONTENTS

Contents

INTRODUCTION TO THE SERIES

ake up and live! No one is destined to be unhappy, consumed with fear and worry, live in poverty, suffer ill health, and feel rejected and inferior. God created all humans in His image and has given us the power to overcome adversity and attain happiness, harmony, health and prosperity.

You have within yourself the power to enrich your life! How to do this is no secret. It has been preached, written about and practiced for millennia. You will find it in the books of the ancient philosophers. All of the great religions have preached it. It is in the Hebrew Scriptures, The Christian Gospels, the Greek philosophers, the Muslim Koran, the Buddhist sutras, the Hindu Bhavad Gita, and the writings of Confucius and Lao Tse. You will find it in the works of modern psychologists and theologians.

This is the basis of the philosophy of Dr. Joseph Murphy, one of the great inspirational writers and lecturers of the twentieth century. He was not just a clergyman, but also a major figure in the modern interpretation of scriptures and other religious writings. As Minister-Director of the Church of Divine Science in Los Angeles, his lectures and sermons were attended by 1,300 to 1,500 people every Sunday. Millions of people tuned in his daily radio program. He wrote over 30 books. His most famous book, *The Power of Your Subconscious Mind*, first published in 1963, became an immediate best seller. It was acclaimed as one of the best self-help guides ever written. Millions of copies have been sold and continue to be sold all over the world.

Following the success of this book, Dr. Murphy lectured to thousands of people in several countries. In his lectures he pointed out how real people have radically improved their lives by applying specific aspects of his concepts and provided practical guidelines on how all people can enrich their lives.

Dr. Joseph Murphy was a proponent of the New Thought movement. This movement was developed in the late nineteenth and early twentieth century by many philosophers and deep thinkers who studied this phenomenon and preached, wrote and practiced a new way of looking at life. By combining a metaphysical, spiritual and pragmatic approach to the way we think and live, they uncovered the secret of attaining what we truly desire.

This philosophy was not a religion in the traditional sense, but it was based on an unconditional belief in a higher being, an eternal presence, God. It was called by various names such as "New Thought" and "New Civilization."

The proponents of the New Thought or New Civilization preached a new idea of life that brings out new methods and more perfected results. They base their thinking on the concept that the human soul is linked with the atomic mind of universal substance, which links our lives with the universal law of supply and we have the power to use it to enrich our lives. To achieve our goals, we must work for it, and this working, we may suffer the thorns and heartaches of humankind. We can do all these things only as we have found the law and worked out the understanding of the law, which God seemed to have written in riddles in the past.

The New Thought concept can be summed up in these words:

You can become what you want to be.

All that we achieve and all that we fail to achieve is the direct result of our own thoughts. In a justly ordered universe, where loss of balance would mean total destruction, individual responsibility must be absolute. Our weaknesses and strengths, purity and impurity are ours alone and that of another person. They are brought about by ourselves and not by another. They can only be altered by ourselves, never by another. All our happiness and suffering are evolved from within. As we think, so we are; as we continue to think, so we remain. The only way we can rise, conquer and achieve is by lifting up our thoughts. The only reason we may remain weak, abject and miserable is to *refuse* to lift up our thoughts.

All achievements, whether in the business, intellectual or spiritual world are the result of definitely directed thought, are governed by the same law and are of the same method; the only difference lies in the object of attainment. Those who would accomplish little must sacrifice little; those who would achieve must sacrifice much; those who would attain a great deal must sacrifice a great deal.

New Thought means a new life: a way of living that is healthier, happier, and more fulfilling in every possible manner and expression. The "New Life" is predicted on age-old, universal laws of mind, and the way of infinite spirituality within the heart and mind of everyone.

Actually, there is nothing new in New Thought, for it is as old and time-honored as humankind. It is new to us when we discover the truths of life that set us free from lack, limitation, and unhappiness. At that moment, New Thought becomes a reoccurring, expanding awareness of the creative power within, of mind-principle, and of our divine potential to be, to do, and to express more of our individual and natural abilities, aptitudes, and talents. Central to mind-principle is that new thoughts, ideas, attitudes, and beliefs create new conditions. According to our beliefs is it done unto us—good, bad, or indifferent. The essence of New Thought consists of the continuing renewing of our mind, that we may prove what is good, and acceptable, and the perfect will of God.

To prove is to know surely, and to have trustworthy knowledge and experience of. The truths of New Thought are practical, easy to demonstrate, and within the realm of accomplishment of everyone—if, and when, he or she chooses. All that is required is an open mind and a willing heart: open to hearing old truth presented in a new and different way, willing to change and to relinquish old, outmoded beliefs, and to accept new ideas and concepts—to have a higher vision of life, or a healing presence within.

The renewing of our mind constitutes the entire purpose and practice of New Thought. Without this on-going, daily renewal, there can be no change. Real New Thought establishes and realized and entirely new attitude, and new consciousness, which inspires and enables us to enter into "life more abundant."

We have within us limitless power to choose, to decide, and our complete freedom to do so—to be conformed, or to be transformed. To be conformed is to live according to that which already has taken or has been given form—that which is visible and apparent to our own senses, ideas, opinions, beliefs, and edicts of others. To be conformed is to live and to be governed "by the fleeting and unstable fashions and conditions of the moment." The very word *conformed* suggests our present environment has form, and we do not, should not, deny its existence. All around us there are injustices, improprieties, and inequalities. We may, we do, find ourselves involved in them at times, and we should face them with courage, and honesty, and do our best to resolve them with integrity and the intelligence which we posses now.

The world accepts and believes, generally, that our environment is the cause of our present condition and circumstance—that the usual reaction and tendency is to drift into a state of acquiescence and quiet acceptance of the present. This is conformity of the worst kind: the consciousness of defeatism. Worse, because it is self-imposed. It is giving all power, and attention, to the outer, manifested state. The outer environment, surroundings, and to the past—by choice and by decision—by the lack of knowledge of the functioning of our wonderful and primary faculty: creative power of the mind, and imagination, is directed toward our goals and aspirations. New Thought insists on the renewal of the mind, and the recognition, and acknowledgment of our responsibility in life—our ability to respond to the truths we now know.

One of the most active and effective of New Thought teachers, Charles Fillmore, co-founder of Unity School or Christianity, was a firm believer in personal responsibility.

In his book, *The Revealing Word*, he wrote (simple, and without equivocation), "Our consciousness is our real environment. The outer environment is always in correspondence to our consciousness."

Anyone who is open and willing to accept the responsibility has begun the transformation—the renewal of the mind that enables us to participate in our transformed life. "To transform" is: "To change from one condition or state to another." (Which is qualitatively better and more fulfilling), "from lack to abundance; loneliness to companionship; limitation to fullness; illness to vibrant health"—through this indwelling wisdom and power, the healing presence will remain within.

True and granted, there are some things we cannot change: the movement of planets, the change in seasons, the pull of the oceans and tides, and the apparent rising and setting of the sun. Neither can we change the minds and thoughts of another person—but we can change ourselves.

Who can prevent or inhibit the movement of your mind, imagination, and your will? Only you can give that power to another. You can be transformed by the renewing of your mind. "This is the key to a new life. Your mind is a recording machine, and all the beliefs, impressions, opinions, and ideas accepted by you are impressed in your deeper, subconscious mind. But you can change your mind. You can begin now to fill your mind with noble and God-like patterns of thoughts, and align yourself with the infinite spirit within. Claim beauty, love, peace, wisdom, creative ideas, and the infinite will respond accordingly, transforming your mind, body, and circumstances. Your thought is the medium between your spirit, your body, and the material.

The transformation begins as we meditate, think upon, and absorb into our mentality those qualities that we desire to experience and to express. Theoretical knowledge is good and necessary. We should know what we're doing, and why. However, actual transformation depends entirely on stirring up the gifts within—the invisible, and intangible, spiritual power given fully to every one of us.

This, and only this, ultimately breaks up and dissolves the very real claims and bondage of past unhappiness and distress. In addition, it heals the wounds of heartbreak and emotional pain. We all desire, and require, peace of mind—the greatest gift—in order to bring it into our environment. Mentally, and emotionally, contemplate divine peace, filling our mind and heart, our entire being. First say, "Peace be unto this house."

To contemplate lack of peace, disharmony, unhappiness, discord, and expect peace to manifest is to expect the apple seed to grow into a pear. It makes little or no sense; it violates all sense of reason. But it is the way of the world. To achieve this we must seek ways to change our minds—to repent—where necessary. As a result, renewal and transformation will occur, following as a natural result. It is desirable and necessary to transform our lives by ceasing to conform to the world's way of choosing, or deciding, according to the events already formed and manifested—to begin to determine the cause behind the physical event—and man-made doctrine, dogma, and ritual—to enter the inner realm of the metaphysical, real New Thought.

The word *metaphysical* has become a synonym for the modern, organized movement. It was first used by Aristotle. Considered by some to have been his greatest writing—his 13th Volume was simply entitled, *Metaphysics*. The dictionary definition is: "beyond natural science; the science of pure being." *Meta-* means "above, or beyond." *Metaphysics*, then, means "above or beyond physics"—"above or beyond the physical:" the world of form. "Meta" is above that, meta- is the spirit of the mind. Behind all things is meta—the mind.

Biblically, the spirit of God is good. "They that worship God worship the spirit, or truth." When we have the spirit of goodness, truth, beauty, love, and goodwill, it is actually God in us, moving through us. God, truth, life, energy, spirit—can it not be defined? How can it be defined? "To define it is to limit it."

This is expressed in a beautiful, old meditation:

Ever the same in my innermost being: eternal, absolutely one, whole, complete, perfect; I AM indivisible, timeless, shapeless, ageless—without face, form, or

figure. I AM the silent brooding presence, fixed in the
hearts of all men (and women)."

We must believe and accept that whatever we imagine and feel to be true will come to pass; whatever we wish for another, we are wishing for ourselves.

Emerson wrote: "We are what we think all day long." In other words and most simply stated: Spirit, thought, mind, and meta is the expression of creative presence and power—and as in nature (physical laws), any power can be used two ways. For example water can clean us or drown us; electricity can provide power that makes life easier or more deadly. The Bible says: "I form the light, and create darkness; I make peace, and evil; I, the Lord, do all these things—I wound, I heal; I bless, I curse."

No angry deity is punishing us, we punish ourselves by misuse of the mind. We also are blessed (benefited) when we comprehend this fundamental principle, and presence, and learn and accept a new thought or an entire concept.

Metaphysics, then, is the study of causation—concerned not with the effect, or the result, which is now manifest, but rather with that which is causing the effect, or the result. Metaphysics approaches spiritual ideas as scientists approach the world of form. Just as they investigate the mind or causation from which the visible is formed, or derived from. If a mind is changed, or a cause is changed, the effect is changed.

The strength and beauty of metaphysics, in my opinion, is that it is not confined to any one particular creed, but it is universal. One can be a Jew, Christian, Muslim, Buddhist, and yet still be a metaphysician.

There are poets, scientists, and philosophers who claim no creed; their belief is metaphysical.

Jesus was a master metaphysician—he understood the mind and employed it to lift up, inspire, and heal others.

When the Mahatma Gandhi (the "great-souled" one) was asked what his religion was, he replied, "I am a Christian . . . a Jew . . . a Buddhist . . . a Hindu . . . I AM all these things."

The phrase *New Thought* has become a popular, generalized term. Comprised of a very large number of churches, centers, prayer groups, and institutions this has become a metaphysical movement which reveals the oneness or unity of humankind with infinite life, the innate dignity and worth, or value, of every individual. In fact, and in truth, in New Thought, the emphasis is toward the individual, rather than an organizational body or function. But, as we said, there is nothing new in New Thought. Metaphysics actually is the oldest of all religious approaches. It reveals our purpose to express God, and the greater measures of the Good. "I AM come to bring you life and that more abundantly." It reveals our identity: "Children of the infinite"—That we are loved and have spiritual value as necessary parts of the Creative Holy (whole) One.

Metaphysics enables and assists us to return to our Divine Source, and ends the sense of separation and feeling of alienation, of wandering in a barren, unfriendly desert wasteland.

Metaphysics has always been, is now, and ever will be available to all—ever patiently waiting our discovery and revelation.

Many thousands have been introduced to New Thought through one or another of its advocates. Its formation was gradual, and usually considered to have begun with Phineas P. Quimby. In a fascinating article in *New Thought* magazine, Quimby wrote about his work in 1837. After experimenting with mesmerism for a period of years, he concluded that it was not the hypnotism itself, but the conditioning of the subconscious mind that led to the resulting changes. Although Quimby had very little formal education, he had a brilliant, investigative mind, and was a very original thinker. In addition to this, he was a prolific writer and diarist. Records have been published detailing the development of his findings. He eventually became a wonderful student of the Bible. He duplicated two-thirds of the Old and New Testament healings. He found that there was much confusion about the true meaning of many biblical passages which caused misunderstanding and misinterpretation of Jesus Christ in the Bible.

All through the twentieth century so many inspired teachers, authors, ministers, and lecturers contributed to the New Thought movement. Dr. Chas E. Braden, of the University of Chicago, called these people "Spirits in Rebellion" because these men and women were truly spirits in rebellion to existing dogmatism, rituals, and creeds. Rebelling at inconsistencies caused the fear of religion. Dr. Braden became no longer content with status quo, and refused any longer to conform.

New thought is an individual practice of the truths of life—a gradual, containing process. We can learn a bit today, and even more tomorrow. Never will we experience a point where there can be nothing more to be discovered. It is infinite, boundless, and eternal. We have all the time we need—eternity. Many are impatient with themselves, and with what they consider failures. Looking back, though, we discover that there have been periods of learning, and we needn't make these mistakes again. Progress may seem ever so slow—"In patience, possess ye your soul."

In Dr. Murphy's book, *Pray Your Way Through It: The Revelation*, he commented that Heaven was noted as being "awareness," and Earth, "manifestation." Your new heaven is your new point of view—your new dimension of consciousness. When we see, that is see *spiritually*, we then realize that in the absolute, all is blessed, harmony, boundless love, wisdom, absolute peace, perfection. Identify with these truths, calm the sea of fear, confidence, faith, and become stronger and surer.

In the books in this series, Dr. Murphy has synthesized the profundities of this power and has put it into an easily understood and pragmatic form so that you can apply it immediately in your life. This book and the others in this series consist of a compilation of lectures, sermons and radio addresses in which Dr. Murphy discussed the techniques of maximizing your potential through the power of the subconscious mind. As Dr. Murphy was a Protestant minister, many of his examples and citations come from the Bible. The concepts these citations illustrate should not be viewed as sectarian. Indeed, the messages conveyed by them are universal and are preached in most religions and philosophies. He often reiterated that the essence of knowledge is in the law of life, the law of belief. It is not Catholic, Protestant, Muslim, or Hindu belief. It is pure and simple belief. "Do unto others accordingly."

His wife, Dr. Jean Murphy, continued his ministry after his death in 1981. In a lecture she gave in 1986, quoting her late husband, she reiterated his philosophy:

> I want to teach men and women of their Divine Origin, and the powers regnant within them. I want to inform that this power is within and that they are their own saviors and capable of achieving their own salvation. This is the message of the Bible and nine-tenths of our confusion today is due to wrongful, literal interpretation of the life-transforming truths offered in it.

I want to reach the majority, the man on the street, the woman overburdened with duty and suppression of her talents and abilities. I want to help others at every stage or level of consciousness to learn of the wonders within.

She said of her husband: "He was a practical mystic, possessed by the intellect of a scholar, the mind of a successful executive, the heart of the poet. His message summed up was: "You are the king, the ruler of your world for you are one with God."

Dr. Murphy was a firm believer that it was God's plan for people to be healthy, prosperous and happy. He countered those theologians and others who claimed desire was evil and urged people to crush out all desire. He said that extinction of desire means apathy—no feeling, no action. He preached that desire is a gift of God. It is all right to desire. It is health and wholesome to desire to become more and better than we were yesterday. Desire for health, abundance, companionship and security. How could these be wrong?

Desire is behind all progress. Without desire nothing would be accomplished. It is the creative power and must be channeled constructively. For example, if poor, desire for wealth wells up from within; if ill, desire for health, lonely, desire for companionship, for love.

We must believe we can improve our lives. A belief—whether it is true, false or merely indifferent—sustained

over a period of time becomes assimilated and is incorporated into our mentality. Unless countermanded by belief
of an opposite nature, sooner or later takes form and is
expressed or experienced as fact, form, condition, circumstance, events of life. We have the power within us to
change negative beliefs to positive ones and thereby change
our lives for the better.

You give the command and your subconscious mind
will faithfully obey it. You will get a reaction or response
from your subconscious mind according to the nature of
the thought you hold in your conscious mind. Psychologists
and psychiatrists point out that when thoughts are conveyed to your subconscious mind, impressions are made in
the brain cells. As soon as your subconscious accepts any
idea, it proceeds to put it into effect immediately. It works
by association of ideas and uses every bit of knowledge that
you have gathered in your lifetime to bring about its purpose. It draws on the infinite power, energy and wisdom
within you. It lines up all the laws of nature to get its way.
Sometimes it seems to bring about an immediate solution
to your difficulties, but at other times it may take days,
weeks or longer.

The habitual thinking of your conscious mind establishes deep grooves in your subconscious mind. This is very
favorable for you if your habitual thoughts are harmonious,
peaceful and constructive. On the other hand, if you have
indulged in fear, worry, and other destructive forms of think-

ing, the remedy is to recognize the omnipotence of your subconscious mind and decree freedom, happiness, perfect health and prosperity. Your subconscious mind, being creative and one with your divine source, will proceed to create the freedom and happiness that you have earnestly decreed.

Now for the first time Dr. Murphy's lectures have been combined, edited and updated in six new books that bring his teachings into the 21st Century. To enhance and augment Dr. Murphy's original lectures, we have incorporated material from some of Dr. Jean Murphy's lectures and have added examples of people whose success reflects Dr. Murphy's philosophy.

The books in this series are:

- *Maximize Your Potential Through the Power of Your Subconscious Mind for a More Spiritual Life*

- *Maximize Your Potential Through the Power of Your Subconscious Mind for an Enriched Life*

- *Maximize Your Potential Through the Power of Your Subconscious Mind for Health and Vitality*

- *Maximize Your Potential Through the Power of Your Subconscious Mind to Create Wealth and Success*

- *Maximize Your Potential Through the Power of Your Subconscious Mind to Develop Self Confidence and Self Esteem*

- *Maximize Your Potential Through the Power of Your Subconscious Mind to Overcome Fear and Worry*

Just reading these books will not improve your life. To truly maximize your potential, you must study these principles, take them to heart, integrate them into your mentality and apply them as an integral part of your approach to every aspect of your life.

Arthur R. Pell, Ph.D.
Editor
May 2005

PREFACE

All people experience times when fear and worry dominate their lives. It may be global factors such as war, famine, political unrest or natural disasters. It may be personal: we or people close to us are besieged with illness, unemployment, overwhelming debts, marital discord, or concern about our children.

These traumas often overwhelm us and remove all joy and happiness from our lives. We cannot always prevent disasters from happening or find immediate solutions to others, but all of us have within us the ability to deal with them so that they will not devastate our lives.

In this book, Dr. Murphy teaches how by prayer and meditation you can develop the power to meet the problems you face and to defeat the depression that usually accompanies them. Pragmatic solutions must still be found, but applying Dr. Murphy's suggestions can often accelerate the process and certainly will enable you to deal more effectively with them.

An illness will still require medical therapies; if you lose a job, you must find another one; if you have legal problems, an attorney can be of aid. Dr. Murphy does not advocate depending on God to cure your illness, find you a job or solve your legal or other problems. But by turning to God, you can keep up your morale, and as he shows over and over again in the examples and anecdotes in his books, God works in mysterious ways and often brings solutions to their problems to believers.

In all of Dr. Murphy's writings, he recommends prayers and mediations that have proven to be effective. In this book, he turns to the psalms as a wonderful source of inspiration and help in overcoming worry and fear.

Psalms have been an important part of Judeo-Christian worship for thousands of years. The inner, esoteric meaning of the psalms reveals the Infinite Healing Power within. The Book of Psalms is sometimes called, "The Little Bible." It is a treasure house of spiritual and practical riches—a great source of inspiration and comfort to all men and women, in every walk of life.

The Book of Psalms addresses our every possible mood, from the depths of despair to height of exultation. In no other single book of the world's holy books, will we find so many varieties of experience—spiritual and secular.

There are psalms of gladness, peace of mind, happiness, joy; wonder and glory of creation, mankind's place in the universe. But there are also cries of the broken heart: in times of sickness, injury, grief, humiliation, share, reproach; treachery or danger; betrayal by friends, associates. And psalms also have been written concerning national peril, as well as personal endangerment, risk.

The variety of moods and attitudes as we approach life, God, encompasses the human experience: From self-pity, loneliness, complaint, despair, sadness, humility, longing, vengeance, smugness to joy, thanksgiving, faith and spiritual ecstasy. When we feel and trill with sense of being at one with life, God, universe, in tune with your personal world.

All these moods and more are addressed in the Little Bible. For this reason, it has been said that every person can discover his or her identity in the Psalms, at any given moment, in all circumstances, every mood: It gives us the sense and feeling that we are indeed a son or daughter of God, a child of the Infinite eternal presence, the living presence of living God, a necessary needed expression of Infinite life.

The Psalms allow us to enter into conversation with our true self, and help us to relate to it. It is we, talking and we, hearing: God speaking through us and in us.

The 150 psalms are, of course, from the Old Testament, which was written in ancient Hebrew and has been translated into most languages. As in any translation, there are variations in what the actual meaning of any word or phrase may be. There are several English language translations of the Bible. In this book Dr. Murphy uses the language of the King James Version, probably the most familiar one. He also points out that the words of the Bible are symbolic and should not be taken literally. The meaning of the symbolism is explained in the text.

Psalms are not the only sources for mediations. Several other prayers and meditations are offered in the book that can help the readers in their efforts to overcome worry and restore to their lives peace of mind.

CHAPTER ONE

Overcoming Worry

Prolonged worry robs you of vitality, enthusiasm and energy and leaves you a physical and mental wreck. Psychosomatic doctors point out that chronic worry is behind numerous diseases such as asthma, allergies, cardiac trouble, high blood pressure and a host of other illnesses too numerous to mention.

The worried mind is confused, divided and is thinking aimlessly about a lot of things that are not true. Worry, really, is due to indolence, laziness, apathy and indifference; because when you wake up, you do not have to think these types of thoughts. You can think of harmony, peace, beauty, right action, love and understanding. You can supplant the negative thought with a constructive thought.

Your problem is in your mind. You have a desire, the realization of which would solve your problem. But when you look at conditions and circumstances as they are, a negative thought comes to your mind and your desire is in conflict with your fear. Your worry is your mind's acceptance of the negative conditions. Realize that your desire is the gift of God. God is the Living Spirit within you. It's telling you to rise higher in life. It's also saying there is no power to challenge God, the Living Spirit within you. There is only One Power; not two, three or four. Just One: That Power moves as unity, as harmony and peace. There are no divisions and quarrels in it. The Almighty Power is now backing me up, revealing to me the perfect plan for its development; and I rest in that conviction."

When worry thoughts come to your mind, remind yourself that Infinite Intelligence is bringing your desire, ideal, plan or purpose to pass in Divine order. That's supplanting the negative thought. Continue in this attitude of mind and the day will break and the shadows will flee away.

After one of my lectures, one of the attendees asked my advice. He had been worried about his health, but after a comprehensive physical exam, his doctor had told him there was nothing wrong with him physically but that he was suffering from anxiety and neurosis. *Anxiety neurosis* is a $25 term for just plain, chronic worry. And the word *worry*, when you translate it from its original root means "to strangle, to choke," which is what that man was doing to himself.

He told me that he was constantly worrying about money, his business and the future. His vision of success and prosperity was thwarted by his chronic worry and the fretting consumed his energy. He felt constantly tired and depressed.

I suggested that he have quiet sessions with himself three or four times a day and declare solemnly that the Almighty has given him inspiration and hope and all he need do is tune in on the Infinite and let the harmony, peace and love of the Infinite move through him. I told him to affirm to himself:

"God, or the Supreme Wisdom, gave me this desire. The Almighty Power is within me, enabling me to be, to do and to have. This Wisdom and Power of the Almighty backs me up and enables me to fulfill all my goals. I think about the Wisdom and Power of the Almighty regularly and systematically. And I no longer think about obstacles, delays, impediments and failure. I know that thinking constantly along this line builds up my faith and confidence and increases my strength and poise, for God hath not given us the spirit of fear but of power, and of love, and of a sound mind."

Sometime later he wrote to me that he continued to do this regularly and systematically. These truths entered into his conscious mind, and then the brain sent these healing vibrations all over his system. They go into his subconscious mind and, like spiritual penicillin; they destroy the bacteria of worry, fear, anxiety and all these negative thoughts. In a month's time he arrived at that awareness of strength, power and intelligence that were Divinely implanted in him at his birth. He has conquered his worries by partaking of spiritual medicine of the Supreme Wisdom and Infinite Intelligence locked in your subconscious depths.

A concerned mother visited me saying that she was terribly worried about her daughter who had joined the Peace Corps and was now in a remote and dangerous area in Africa. I gave her a specific prayer to use night and morning for herself and for her daughter. A year later her daughter completed her tour in Africa safely and returned home and married her long-time boyfriend.

Again the mother came to see me, just as worried as before. She was again concerned about her daughter. She was worried during the second visit that her daughter may have married the wrong man; however, she admitted that the man was a wonderful husband. "When she became pregnant I was so worried that their child might be born dead or crippled. But my daughter has given birth to a perfect child." She was also worried about a money shortage in her daughter's home. This woman was not really worried about what she *thought* she was worried about.

Her actual difficulty was that she had an inward sense of insecurity. She was emotionally immature and, certainly, spiritually immature. If she was spiritually mature, she would have sat down, blessed her son-in-law and daughter, realizing God was guiding them, there was right action in their lives, Divine law and order govern them, and Divine peace fills their soul. That God was prospering them beyond their fondest dreams. How, then, could she be worried about them?

She was just an anxious person. Her real problem was that she was not in tune with the Infinite, Her thoughts were not God's thoughts.

When your thoughts are God's thoughts, God's power is with your thoughts of good. It's as simple as that. You must cleanse your mind like you cleanse out your own home. If you don't keep the house clean, all sorts of pestiferous insects come in, the paint falls off of the walls, and all manner of things begin to happen. The mind is your house. You have to keep constantly cleaning it, filling it with truths of God, which crowd out of the mind everything unlike God.

While talking to her I was able to show her that she was the creator of her own worries. She thereupon replaced her inner sense of insecurity with a real feeling of security. I wrote out a special prayer for her to use. It is taken from the 91st Psalm, the great Psalm of protection. If you are an anxious person, use this prayer

"He that dwelleth in the secret place of the Most High shall abide under the shadow of the Almighty mind. All the thoughts entertained by me conform to harmony, peace and goodwill. That's discipline. My mind

is the dwelling place of happiness, joy and a deep sense of security. All the thoughts that enter my mind contribute to my joy, peace and general welfare. I live, move and have my being in the atmosphere of good fellowship, love and unity. All the people that dwell in my mind (people that dwell in your mind are thoughts, ideas, images, feelings, emotional reaction, and so forth) *are God's children, meaning they are God's ideas. I am at peace in my mind with all the members of my family and with all mankind. The same good I wish for myself I wish for my daughter and her family. I am living in the house of God now. I claim peace and happiness, for I know I dwell in the house of the Lord forever."*

She reiterated these truths frequently during the day, and these wonderful spiritual vibrations neutralized and obliterated the disease-soaked worry center in her subconscious mind, which is like a psychic wound, festering, traumatic wound. She discovered that there were spiritual reserves on which she could call to annihilate the negative thoughts. As she saturated her mind with these wonderful, spiritual verities, she became possessed by a deep faith in all things good. She is now living in the joyous expectancy of the best.

There are many prayers that can help you overcome worry. Every morning before the day's work go to a quiet place and identify yourself mentally and emotionally with these truths:

> "*I live, move and have my being in God* (God is the Life Principle in you, and you know very well you are alive; and God is the Progenitor or the Father of all, so all religions of the world say 'Our Father'). *God lives, moves and has His being in me. I AM the temple of the Living God. God lives in me. I am immersed in the Divine Presence Which surrounds me, enfolds me and enwraps me. My mind is God's mind and my Spirit is the Spirit of God. This Infinite Being within me is the Only Presence and the Only Power. It cannot be defeated, thwarted or frustrated in any way. There is nothing to oppose It, challenge It, thwart It or neutralize It. It's Almighty. It moves as unity. There are no divisions or quarrels in It. It is all powerful and all wise.*
>
> *It is present everywhere. As I unite mentally with this Infinite Power through my thoughts, I know I am greater than any problem. I grapple courageously with all difficulties and problems knowing they are Divinely outmatched, and whatever strength, power and creative ideas I need will automatically be given to me by the Divine Intelligence within me. I know the Infinite lies stretched in smiling repose within me, where all is bliss, harmony and peace. I am now in tune with*

the Infinite, and its wisdom, power and intelligence become active and potent in my life. This is the law of my being, and I know God's peace fills my soul. I know I can't think of two things at the same time. I can't think of failure and dwell upon success at the same time in my mind."

Do you shovel out the darkness in your own home? No, you turn on the light. And the light dissipates the darkness. Like the sun dissipates the mist. And darkness is absence of light. All you have to do is turn on the light in your own mind. You can say, "I dwell in the secret place of the Most High. I abide in the shadow of the Almighty. I will say of the Lord, He is my refuge and my fortress: my God, in Him will I trust. He covers me with His feathers, and under His wing shall I rest. The truth is my shield and buckler." Isn't that a wonderful thing to say? Isn't it a wonderful thing to affirm? Isn't it a marvelous thing to know? Isn't it a wonderful, wonderful thing to practice it and all the worry will go away.

A truck driver came to see me. He was panicked. He had two bad accidents and he knew that if he had one more accident he would be discharged from his job. Each time he climbed into the cab of his truck, he quaked with fear. I told him he could not fear his journey and bless his trip at the same moment. Therefore, he had to supplant his worry with confidence and a sense of security. He began each trip by blessing himself and his truck as follows:

"I am Divinely guided in all my ways. Divine love goes before me making joyous and perfect my way. My truck is God's truck. This guides me and directs me in all my movements. Divine law and order govern me in my driving, and I go from town to town freely, joyously and lovingly. I bless all other drivers on the road. I wish for them health, happiness and peace, and right action. I am an ambassador of God. I know that all the parts of my vehicle are God's idea and function perfectly. I am always poised, serene and calm. I am always alert, alive and quickened by the Holy Spirit. This love surrounds me and goes before me making straight, joyous and perfect my way. I am always surrounded by the sacred circle of God's eternal love, and Divine love goes before me making straight, joyous and wonderful my way."

During the past three years he has had no accident, and he has received no citations or traffic violation tickets. He began to fill his mind with these truths and crowded out of his mind all worry thoughts that had haunted him. He said, "I made it a habit to use that prayer all the time I was on the road. I committed the whole thing to memory. It was not mumbo jumbo. I knew what I was doing and why I was doing it. I knew I was implanting these ideas in my subconscious, and whatever is impressed on the subconscious comes forth as form, function, experience and events. I also knew that the higher vibration of my spiritual thoughts would wipe out the lower vibration."

This truck driver is no longer worried or fearful. He knows that prayer changes things. This is discipline, of course. Prayer is a habit—a very good habit. How did you learn to walk? You made many attempts to walk across the floor. You fell down. You had a thought pattern. You began to move your legs and so forth. Gradually, it became second nature when you walked across the floor. In other words, if you repeat a thought pattern or act over and over again, after a while it becomes second nature, which is the response of your subconscious mind to your conscious thinking and acting. And that's prayer, too.

I was in a store in Wichita a few years ago. The proprietor invited me to come back of the counter where he showed me a sign over the cash register: "I will fear no evil for thou art with me." (That's from the 23rd Psalm.) He added that the store had been robbed three times, and he had been held up twice with a gun pointed at his head.

He said, "After the third robbery I wanted to sell the store and get into some other trade, but I had so much invested in the store—not only in money, but in the long-term relationships with my customers and my love of the community that I decided to stay. I prayed hard over it. I read and reread my bible and was comforted and encouraged by what I read, especially the 23rd psalm.

"I think of that sentence of the Psalm, and it falls as a blessing on my mind. I have taken this Infinite Presence and Power within me as my partner, and I claim many times during the day, 'The Infinite Intelligence within me is my higher self; It's my senior partner. This Intelligence guides me and watches over me. His power and wisdom are instantly available to me. I am not alone.' Now I feel secure, because I know God's circle of love surrounds this store, myself and all of my customers. I make this prayer a habit: 'I will fear no evil for thou art with me. Thy rod and thy staff, they comfort me. Goodness and mercy follow me all the days of my life, for I dwell in the house of God forever.'"

The house of God is your own mind. Your mind is where you walk and talk with God, for God is that Supreme Intelligence, that Boundless Wisdom within you. It's locked in your own subconscious depths.

The storekeeper met the problem of anxiety and worry, and he overcame it. During the past four years he has had no trouble and has prospered beyond his fondest dreams. He realized that his worry was irrational thought. There is an Infinite Intelligence and Boundless Wisdom, which we call God knocking at the door of your heart. It opens with an inside latch. All you have to do is let it in and contact it with your thought. It will lift you up, heal you, inspire you, guide you, and open for you new doors of expression, watch over you, sustain you. That's the Presence and Power that heals a cut on your finger. If you burn yourself it reduces the edema and gives you new skin and tissue. It's that which started your heartbeat and watches over you when you are sound asleep.

Now, it's just the same as if it were not there except you use It. That's why I say that worry is laziness.

An engineer told me how he overcomes all his worries. He looks at them as an engineering problem. "When I face a technical problem on the job," he said, "I take it apart and break it into small pieces. Then I ask myself 'Where do they come from?' 'What does each piece signify?' 'How can I adapt it to the entire problem?' With worries I ask 'Do these worries have any power?' 'Is there any principle behind them?'"

With his cool, rational thought and logical analysis, he dismembers his worries and realizes they are shadows in his mind, fallacious and illusionary. No reality, just shadows in the mind.

A shadow has no power! Well, that's what worry is: a shadow in your mind. It has no reality, no principle behind it, no truth behind it. These worries are no more than a conglomeration of sinister shadows.

Doctors will tell you that many of their patients worry so much about diseases that they do not have, that they suffer the symptoms of that ailment. Doctors call this *psychosomatic*: The roots of this word are "psycho," which means of the mind and "somatic," meaning of the body. What you think in your mind is reflected by the reaction of your body.

A friend of mine, the assistant pastor of a church in Los Angeles was worried that he had a bad heart. His senior pastor, a man twenty years older than he, had just had a heart attack and he was sure that he was also susceptible. He went to see a heart specialist, who took a cardiogram and learned that his heart was normal and that his problem was psychosomatic. The senior pastor's heart attack triggered in him an inordinate concern about his own heart and he actually experienced spasms in his chest and other symptoms of heart trouble. The doctor told him: "You should practice what you preach. The cure for your problem is not in my medical books, but in the Book of Books. Read again and again the 27th Psalm. Meditate on it until the false idea is lifted from your psych and your soma will respond."

It only took a few weeks. He practiced the great law of substitution by repeating the good idea over and over again until the mind lays hold of the truth, which sets him free.

It takes a little work, but you can do it. That's why I said it is discipline. It's a willingness to do it. "I'm going to overcome this. I'm going to meet it head on. It's a shadow in my mind, and I'm not going to give power to shadows." These emotional spasms were caused because he was obsessed with the idea that he had a bad heart. He didn't. He was completely healed. He was healed of what? A false belief in his own mind.

Another example of how prayer and meditation can help overcome worry and restore health was brought to my attention when a man with a seemingly well adjusted and composed personality came to see me. He was very worried and anxious because his personal doctor told him his blood pressure was over 200; that he should take it easy and relaxes more. He said to me, "I can't take it easy. I have too much to do, and the pressure in my organization is terrific." He was really suffering from a long mounting accumulation of petty frustrations and worries.

I suggested that he begin to apply this simple truth to himself: That he could not be sick forever; that he was here to meet all problems and to overcome them, not run away from them; that he is mentally and spiritually equipped to handle any problem, regardless of what it is—meet it head on, grapple with it courageously and say, "The problem is here, but Infinite Intelligence is here, too, and knows only the answer." All conditions, circumstances and events are subject to alteration. Every created thing will some day pass away. The age-old maxim: "This, too, shall pass away," is always true. But your mind and Spirit, the personality of you, will never pass away.

The first step was that he had to extract his attention from his ailment and business difficulties and trust the Creative Intelligence within him, which made his body, to heal and to restore him. I gave him the following meditation to use several times each day accompanied by a suggestion that he was to assert absolutely and believe implicitly the following simple truths:

Periodically during the day I shall withdraw my attention from the vexations and strife of the world and I return to the Divine Presence within me and commune with that Creative Intelligence within. I know I am nourished spiritually and mentally, and God's river of peace floods my mind. Infinite Intelligence reveals to me the perfect idea for every problem I meet. I reject the appearance of things, and I affirm the supremacy of the Presence and Power within me. I am absorbed and engrossed in the great truth that Infinite Intelligence is guiding me, that Divine Right Action reigns supreme. The Miraculous Healing Presence is flowing through me now, permeating every atom of my being. His river of peace flows through my mind and heart, and I am relaxed, poised, serene and calm. I know the Divine Presence Which made me is now restoring me to wholeness and perfection. I give thanks for the miraculous healing which is taking place now.

By affirming regularly many times a day in this manner, he succeeded in retrieving his senses from the annoyances and irritations of the day. In a month's time a medical checkup revealed normal blood pressure. He discovered that his renewed mind restored his body to wholeness. When the strain and pressure of business tend to disturb him today, his motto is: "None of these things moves me." He has that on his desk.

Do things disturb you? If you have no opinion there is no suffering. You have no opinion about the headlines in the newspaper today. Where there is no opinion there is no suffering. If the cucumber is bitter, don't eat it. If there are briars and brambles on the road you are traveling, avoid them.

Tune in on the Infinite. How, then, could you be disturbed? Aren't you disturbing yourself? Exalt Divine wisdom in the midst of you. Say to yourself: "I will lift up mine eyes into the hills from whence cometh my help."

In a Nutshell

When worry thoughts come to your mind, remind yourself that Infinite Intelligence is bringing your desire, ideal, plan or purpose to pass in Divine order. That's supplanting the negative thought.

When your thoughts are God's thoughts, God's power is with your thoughts of good. You must cleanse your mind like you cleanse out your own home. The mind is your house. You have to constantly declutter it, filling it with truths of God, which crowd out of the mind everything unlike God.

If you repeat a thought pattern or act over and over again, after a while it becomes second nature, which is the response of your subconscious mind to your conscious thinking and acting. And that's prayer, too.

The house of God is your own mind. Your mind is where you walk and talk with God, for God is that Supreme Intelligence, that Boundless Wisdom within you. It's locked in your own subconscious depths

All conditions, circumstances and events are subject to alteration. Every created thing will some day pass away. The age-old maxim: "This, too, shall pass away," is always true. But your mind and Spirit, the personality of you, will never pass away.

CHAPTER TWO

Banish Guilt

L ife holds no grudge against anyone. God is the Life Principle within you. It's animating, sustaining, and strengthening you this very moment. If you are wondering where God is, the Life Principle in you is God. It's the Living Spirit Almighty within you. It's your mind, your Spirit. You are alive with the life of God, for God is life and that is your life now. Life is forever forgiving us. We must let the scales of superstition fall from our eyes and become aware of simple truths, which were always known.

Truth has been distorted, twisted, and prostituted beyond recognition. This is why guilt is universal. Psychologists call guilt the curse of curses; yet the Life Principle does not condemn us, we condemn ourselves. In all ages, people have been told to banish their sense of guilt; and they employed various ceremonies and rituals for this purpose.

In ancient times, they sacrificed their bullocks and doves to propitiate a God of wrath. When storms came crops were ruined or a great drought prevailed. The people believed the gods were angry. The tribal priest had to give the people an answer. If he did not give the people an explanation they would kill him. Therefore, the tribal priest gave answers that satisfied the superstitious imaginings of these people.

In ancient times and even now in remote parts of the world people have sacrificed their children to appease the so-called angry gods of fire, flood, and famine. This is somewhat like paying a gangster, giving him tribute every week in order to curry favor with him so he will not throw a bomb in your store.

Now, if you burn your hand, life forgives you, reduces the edema, and gives you new skin, tissue, and cells. Life does not hold a grudge against you. If you injure your hand, cutting it severely, life forgives you. New cells build bridges over the cut and you have a marvelous healing. Life is always forgiving you. Life is giving and forgiving. If you take some bad food, life forgives you, too; causes you to expel and regurgitate it. Life has no ill will against you.

We must learn to use the Life Principle the right way and cease going against the stream of life. When a child is born, it is universal life individualizing itself and appearing in your home. The child has no discrimination or discernment. It has not begun to use its reason as yet. Therefore, it is subject to the mood and attitude of the parents.

Every child wants to follow its own inherent drives. It thinks nothing evil about these things. But the father or mother who does not understand says, "You little brat. You are a sinner. You are evil. You are a naughty girl. God is going to punish you. You are going to suffer for this." The child is baffled. She cannot reason out what is wrong, as she lacks discernment. She, therefore, feels cut off from love, affection, and security, for that is what the mother represents to her. She feels that her mother is angry, and reacts perhaps by wetting her bed at night. Psychologists say that this is his way of indicating that the child wants to drown her mother in resentment The child may also react in this way by becoming timid, weak, and inferior, showing a deep sense of inferiority or rejection.

A young boy might react to a cruel, tyrannical father by becoming hostile, belligerent, and resentful. He knows his father is a big man, so he suppresses his anger. His rage is suppressed, and it becomes a festering sore. Later on he finds himself opposed to authority, because he has been against his father all his young life. He gets in trouble with the police, the professor at school, and other symbols of authority. He is always fighting his father. He does not know it, because no one has ever taught him how his mind works.

Even the president of the United States is subject to authority. Congress has power over him. We all have to live and adjust to authority. Wherever we go there is authority.

We must learn to establish control over our thoughts, feelings, and responses. We must take charge of our own mind. When we do take charge of this motley crew in our mind and say to them, "I am the master, I am going to order my thoughts around," and tell them what to give attention to, then we'll be like an employer ordering employees to execute his instructions.

You must take charge of your own mind; not permit others to govern it for you. Creed, dogma, traditions, superstition, fear, and ignorance rule the mind of the average person. The greatest desert in the world is not the Sahara; it is in the mind of the average person. Average people do not own their own minds at all. Their minds do not belong to them. It is often ruled over by strong-minded family members or governed by domination of others.

We must realize that a great sense of guilt comes from what is called conscience. A great number of people think that the voice of conscience is that of God. It is not. Conscience is your inner feeling and the voice of someone else. Often it is the voice of ignorance, fear, superstition, falsehoods, and weird concepts of a God of love.

I knew a boy who feared that God would punish him because he did not go to church on Sunday. This is the inner voice of superstition and false belief implanted in his subconscious mind by his parents, preachers or teachers. This belief on the part of the boy gave him a sense of guilt, and he felt that he must be punished. When you were young you were given taboos, restrictions, homilies, and a series of "don'ts." You were, perhaps, told that you were evil, a sinner, that you would be punished. Perhaps you were told of a lake of fire waiting for you if you did not behave and believe in a particular creed. The minds of children are contaminated and polluted with all kinds of strange notions and false doctrines.

Children are particularly susceptible to feelings of guilt when they disobey parents or teachers. They are warned that disobedience will lead to punishment—not only by the parents for the specific disobedient act, but God will punish them for being naughty. This can be disastrous to some children. It breeds with in them a guilt complex that can destroy their lives. It would be far better to explain to the child why what they did was wrong, and administer appropriate punishment such as a time-out or a withdrawal of a privilege. Do not invoke the fear of eternal damnation on the child. It is better to tell the child that God's love never ceases and will be there to help him or her live a good life.

Children should never be told that they were born in iniquity and conceived in sin. It's a monstrous lie; it's too stupid for words. They should be taught that they are children of God. As Moses said, "We are all children of the I AM." And that God is their real Father, and that God is love. God is *your* Father, and that is the Life Principle within *you*. It's the Progenitor of all. It's *our* Father. It's the Father of all the people in this world, for there is only one Life Principle.

The children should be taught also that love cannot do anything unloving. Peace cannot wish pain, joy can't wish sadness, and love can't do anything unloving. There are a lot of things God cannot do. God cannot punish you. God cannot wish death, for life cannot wish death. That would be a contradiction of its own nature.

There is the good conscience where the child is taught the Golden Rule, love of others; respect for parents, that honesty is the best policy. When a child is tempted to steal, there is that within him or her that cries out, "No, you shouldn't do that; that belongs to someone else." The mother and father are there to teach the child the difference between rat poison and butter, the difference between the skunk and the cat; the difference between what is right and what is wrong. The child has to go to school. He or she has to learn manners, be indoctrinated properly, and learn what is right, true, noble, and God-like. The child must learn about universal principles, eternal verities, which never change. They are the same yesterday, today, and forever. Yet how many are taught these qualities today? We all want self-esteem, wants to feel worthy, want to be recognized by our neighbors as honest, sincere, and good.

You want your children and your spouse to love you. You want the respect of the community. When you fall short of expressing yourself in doing the right thing, you feel a sense of guilt and proceed to punish yourself.

Some people have serious doubts about their priorities. On one hand they believe that what they are doing is what is best for their families and themselves, but on the other hand, they have qualms about it.

Barbara L. was such a person. She was a very successful real estate sales executive who supervised a staff of seven Realtors and was acclaimed by her company as one of their best producers. She was a single mother of two school-age boys. She made sure they were well taken care of. They attended a prestigious private school, and had a full-time housekeeper who prepared their meals, attended to their needs and drove them to and from school and their many other activities. Barbara often had to work nights and weekends, but tried to make the time she spent with the boys quality time. When she was home, she talked with them, played games and helped them with their homework, but she was not a happy person.

She told me she felt so full of guilt that she was not a good mother. She said: "I must work long hours on my job. I must be available to show clients houses at their convenience, not mine. I depend on my job to support my kids." This strong sense of guilt had become so great that it was affecting her health. He blood pressure had risen well above normal; she had difficulty sleeping and had frequent digestive problems.

I asked her if her children were doing well. "Oh, yes," she responded. "They are both doing well in school. The older boy is on the baseball team and has many friends. The younger is more interested in music and is doing well with his piano and guitar lessons. They love the housekeeper and they are very affectionate with me. I truly believe they are happy."

"If they are happy and doing well, why are you feeling so guilty?" I asked her.

We discussed this and she said. "My mother disapproves of my lifestyle. She was always a stay-at-home mom and strongly believes that a mother's first priority is taking care of the children. I can't disagree. I could get a less demanding job and be home much more, but I am making an income that enables my children to have the best education and care they could get. My mother says God will punish me for not being a good mother and I am concerned that she may be right and I don't know what to do."

I explained that God cannot condemn you, cannot punish you. You do it to yourself. If your let other people take control of your mind, you lose the freedom God has given you to make decisions based on your own thoughts. What you are doing is letting your mother's feelings replace your own feelings in your subconscious and the result is conflict and guilt. Yes, we should honor our parents, as the Bible says, but that does not mean that they are always right. What is right for them may not be right for you. You must follow your own heart—that is your own subconscious mind. You must feed your conscious mind with positive thoughts by prayer and meditation and it will push out from your subconscious the seeds of guilt sown by your mother. Post the following prayer on your mirror so you see it every morning when you rise and every night before you retire:

The kingdom of God is within me.
Infinite intelligence will lead and guide me
in all my ways when I turn to it and call upon it.

Self-condemnation is the most destructive of all mental poisons. It robs you of vitality, enthusiasm, and energy. It may affect all the organs of your body. If you have a glass of dirty water, you may condemn, resent, and curse it indefinitely. But you will not get clean water. However, if you continually pour clean water into the glass, you will have clean water. No matter what you have done in the past— if you have been a murderer, robbed, cheated, defrauded, committed all manner of evil—if you stop now and change your mind and let Divine love, peace, and harmony flood your mind, and if you are sincere in transforming yourself, the past is forgotten and remembered no more.

From the Mind Principle there is no time or space. If you had misused the laws of chemistry for 50 years, and suddenly you re-studied these laws and brought forth marvelous compounds, do you mean to tell me that the principle of chemistry has a grudge against you because you misused it? Your mind principle is the same as the principle of chemistry. It has no grudge against you. Forgive yourself and walk on.

I have often been asked to provide a comprehensive summary of my concepts on a specific subject by giving my listeners or readers a list of suggestions that synthesize my ideas. Here are ten basic rules on dealing with feelings of guilt:

1. We are not born with a sense of guilt. Guilt is a mental disease and is abnormal and unnatural.

2. What we want must first be conceived in our thoughts and then programmed into our subconscious mind.

3. Conscience is our inner feeling. It is not necessarily based on Truth. It is often the voice of ignorance, fear, superstition, and prejudices implanted in our minds by our parents or by others we look upon as authorities.

4. It is wrong to threaten children by saying "God will punish you." God punishes no one.

5. Don't let your conscience be your guide. Your true guide is God; It is that Infinite Intelligence that will lead you to living a good ("Godlike") life.

6. Different cultures, religions and ethnic groups have different concepts of "conscience."

7. What is "Godlike" is not dictated by any one religion. God knows nothing about creeds, dogma or sectarian opinions. God is above all.

8. God and God alone should be your spiritual guide.

9. Many people are misled and are full of guilt because they accept as right that which is actually wrong.

10. God wants us to be happy. God's law is the law of health, happiness, peace, order, beauty, good deeds and prosperity.

═══ In a Nutshell ═══

We must learn to use the Life Principle the right way and cease going against the stream of life. When a child is born, it is universal life individualizing itself and appearing in your home. The child has no discrimination or discernment. It has not begun to use its reason as yet. Therefore, it is subject to the mood and attitude of the parents.

You must take charge of your own mind; not permit others to govern it for you. Creed, dogma, traditions, superstition, fear, and ignorance rule the mind of the average person. The greatest desert in the world is in the mind of the average person. Average people do not own their own minds at all. Their minds do not belong to them. It is often ruled over by strong-minded family members or governed by domination of others.

Children are particularly susceptible to feelings of guilt when they disobey parents or teachers. They are warned that disobedience will lead to punishment—not only by the parents for the specific disobedient act, but God will punish them for being naughty. This can be disastrous to some children. It breeds with in them a guilt complex that can destroy their lives. Do not invoke the fear of eternal damnation on the child. It is better to tell the child that God's love never ceases and will be there to help him or her live a good life.

If you let other people take control of your mind, you lose the freedom God has given you to make decisions based on your own thoughts. You must follow your own heart—that is your own subconscious mind. You must feed your conscious mind with positive thoughts by prayer and meditation and it will push out from your subconscious the seeds of guilt sown by others,

Self-condemnation is the most destructive of all mental poisons. It robs you of vitality, enthusiasm, and energy.

It may affect all the organs of your body. If you let Divine love, peace, and harmony flood your mind, and if you are sincere in transforming yourself, the past is forgotten and remembered no more.

CHAPTER THREE

The Supreme Mastery of Fear

The most extensive of all the morbid mental conditions which reflect themselves so disastrously on the human system is the state of fear, It may range from the state of extreme alarm, fright, or terror, down to the slightest shade of apprehension of impending evil. But all along the line it is the same thing—a paralyzing impression upon the centers of life that can produce a variety of morbid symptoms in every tissue of the body.

Fear is like a poison gas pumped into one's atmosphere, It causes mental, moral, and spiritual asphyxiation, and sometimes death—death to energy, death to tissue, and death to all growth.

In this chapter we will explore how fear can keep you from success and what you can do to overcome this blight and turn your thoughts from fear to courage. It starts with a strong belief that you and God are one. One with God is a majority; and if God be for me, who can be against me? The Life Principle is always for you. It heals a cut on your finger. If you take some bad food It causes you to regurgitate it. If you burned yourself it reduces the edema, gives you new skin and tissue. It always seeks to preserve you, to heal and restore you.

Keep telling your subconscious you are Divine. Your subconscious wants you to say it over and over again, for ideas are conveyed to the subconscious by repetition, faith and expectancy. Do it again, and again, and again; and realize that the God Presence is within you and that you are one with it. You are Divine. You are a son of the Living God, heir to all of God's riches. And all the power of the God Head flows to your focal point of attention.

There are plenty of people who are simply afraid to live; scared to death for fear they will die. They do not know how to dislodge the monster fear that terrifies them, and it dogs their steps from the cradle to the grave.

For thousands of people, the dread of some impending evil is ever present. It haunts them even in their happiest moments. Their happiness is poisoned with it so that they never take much pleasure or comfort in anything. It is the ghost at the banquet, the skeleton in the closet. It is ingrained into their very lives and emphasized in their excessive timidity, their shrinking, and self-conscious bearing.

Some people are afraid of nearly everything. They are afraid of a draught; afraid of getting chilled or taking cold;

afraid to eat what they want; to venture in business matters for fear of losing their money; afraid of public opinion. They have a perfect horror of what their neighbors think. They are afraid hard times are coming; afraid of poverty; afraid of failure; afraid the crops are going to fail; afraid of lightning and tornadoes. Their whole lives are filled with fear, fear, fear.

Fear and worry make us attract the very things we dread. The fear habit impairs health, shortens life and paralyzes efficiency. Doubt and fear mean failure; faith is an optimist, fear a pessimist.

Fear in all its different phases of expression, such as worry, anxiety, anger, jealousy, timidity, is the greatest enemy of the human race. It has robbed humankind of more happiness and efficiency, has made more people cowards, more people failures or forced them into mediocrity, than anything else.

There is no need to fear. Tell yourself that over and over again. Gradually, your subconscious will accept it. And your subconscious will believe it, because you believe it in your conscious, reasoning mind. Whatever your conscious mind really believes, your subconscious will dramatize and bring to manifestation. Do not vacillate or equivocate. Your subconscious mind knows when you are sincere. It knows when you really believe; then, it will respond.

Tell yourself frequently that God dwells within you, that you are Divine that Omnipotence is moving on your behalf. Say it to yourself when you are challenged, whenever you have any kind of trouble or difficulty. That this is divinely outmatched. The problem is here, but the God Presence is here, too. Say it to yourself when you are driving the car, when you are going to sleep, when you are talking to someone. Realize God is thinking, speaking, acting through you. And realize it is always functioning.

When fear comes, say, "Faith in God opens the door of my mind and there is no one there." Realize you are one with this God Power. You are aligned with it now, and mighty forces will come to your aid. You are one with the Infinite, with life, and with all things.

The Bible says: "Thou shalt compass me about with songs of deliverance. I will fear no evil for Thou art with me. Thy rod and thy staff, they comfort me. Goodness and mercy follow me all the days of my life, for I dwell in the house of God forever." Your mind is the house of God. It's where you walk and talk with the Supreme Intelligence— this Infinite Presence and Power.

When you are fearful or indulge in negative thoughts, you are vibrating at a very low level. When you meditate on a Psalm and say to yourself, "The Lord is my shepherd; I shall not want," or "The Presence of God is right where I am," or "I will fear no evil for God is with me," or "I dwell in the secret place of the Most High and I abide in the shadow of the Almighty," or "I will say of the Lord, He is my refuge, my fortress; my God, in Him will I trust," or "Surely, He will cover me with His feathers, and under His wing shall I rest," or "The truth shall be my shield and buckler."

Affirm frequently: "God is guiding me now. The Presence of God is with me." Then you are thinking spiritually. Your thoughts now are God's thoughts, and all the power of God flows through that thought. That's the meaning of: One with God is a majority. For the only immaterial power is your thought, and your thought is creative. Therefore, think of harmony; think of Infinite love flowing through you, vitalizing, healing, and restoring you. These spiritual thoughts are of a very high frequency and are of a very high vibration.

What happens to the evil, negative thoughts—the fear, foreboding, destruction, disaster, earthquakes, and things of this nature? When you say, "Oh, maybe another earthquake will come; maybe my house will be knocked down," think along these lines:

Say, "God's love surrounds me and enfolds me. The Presence of God is in my home" (which is the presence of harmony, beauty, love and peace). Divine love saturates the walls, the atmosphere. Wherever you are, whether asleep or awake, or walking the streets, or behind the counter, God's love surrounds you, enfolds you and enwraps you. You are immunized; you are God-intoxicated; you have no fear.

You are not afraid of anything in the past, the present or the future. You are not afraid of people, conditions or events. For the Eternal God is your dwelling place and the everlasting arms of wisdom, truth and beauty. You are immersed in the Holy Omnipresence. In Him we live, and move, and have our being. And this God Presence lives, moves, and has His being in us.

Now you are vibrating at a spiritual frequency; and just like you put your finger on a tuning fork, that is the end of the negative or fearful vibration. That is the end of the evil, for evil is a false belief of God, the Infinite One, and the Infinite Goodness of the Infinite One.

When we are full of fear, we have greater faith in evil than in the God Presence. That is shocking, but it's true. Fear is God upside down. You have faith that the sun will rise in the morning; you have faith that you can drive your car; you have faith that you will get an answer to your prayer when you pray for guidance. But many people have faith in the wrong thing. There are people who are looking forward to misfortune. There are people working in offices who are afraid of their jobs. They are afraid they are going to lose their money. And of what is going to happen to them when they grow old, instead of realizing: "I am always in my true place. God is the Source of my supply, and all my needs are met at every moment of time and point of space. God is my instant and everlasting supply, meeting all my needs at every moment of time, no matter where I am. I am always gainfully employed. I am always working for Him, and I live forever."

Why be upset, angry or fearful at another's remark? Does what others say contribute to your success, your happiness, your peace, or your failure in any way? No. Their thoughts have no power. Your power is with your thoughts of good. Someone may spread lies about you. You say, "Oh, well, they are undermining me. They are telling lies about me." And you are full of fear and anger. But does their opinion make it so? No. What governs you? Is it your belief or another's belief? What governs you? Is it your thought or someone else's? Do you own your own mind? Are you permitting others to manipulate you? Who's thinking for you? Are you coming to your own decisions? Are you doing your own thinking?

You are in the kingdom of heaven. The kingdom of heaven means you are king over your conceptive realm, which is your own mind. You have authority, dominion over your thoughts, feelings, emotions and actions. That's why the kingdom of heaven is within you. It's not a place up in the skies where you go; you are already there.

Why make yourself subservient to another's thought? Why not have reverence for your own thought? Your thought is Divine. It is creative. It is of God. The capacity of Spirit is to think. You are a Spirit. When were you not a Spirit? You will always be a Spirit. You are a Spirit now. Have a healthy, reverent respect for your thought, because your thought is your prayer. What you feel, you attract; what you imagine, you become.

Your thought governs you, not another. Stand tall. Stand up straight, and say: "I am one with the Infinite, which lies stretched in smiling repose." The finite alone hath wrought and suffered, but the Infinite lies stretched in smiling repose.

Yes, each time a fear thought comes to you, supplant it and say, "God loves me and cares for me." Say to yourself: "God loves me. The sacred circle of God's eternal love surrounds me. The whole armor surrounds me, and enfolds me, and enwraps me. And Divine love goes before me making straight and perfect my way."

A pilot said to me, "I'm never afraid when I navigate a plane, whether I go north, south, east or west, for I am a pilot for God. I am flying for Him. And I am as safe in the sky as on the earth. Nothing can happen to me. It is impossible. I am always surrounded by the sacred circle of God's eternal love."

Robby Wright, a lad who works in my recording studio is a person of tremendous faith and has a great reverence for things Divine. And whatever he prays for, he gets; because, he said, "The Source is God. Therefore, whatever I pray for, it already is. Because I couldn't think of it if it were not so." Therefore, whether it's an automobile, or a bicycle, or a trip to Europe, or whatever it is he prays for, he realizes that before he calls, the answer is there. And all this lad's prayers are answered in Divine order. He never looks to any person, place, or thing. He looks to the Source. That's a smart young man.

Have faith in the goodness of God, and the right action of God, and the guidance of that Infinite One within you. Have faith in the eternal principles and in the immutable, changeless laws of God. Have faith in your own mind; because any idea that you emotionalize, nourish, sustain, exalt in your mind, by the process of osmosis sinks down into your subconscious where it dies like a seed and bequeaths its energy to another form of itself. And what is the energy that it bequeaths? It is the joy of the answered prayer. After all, the corn and wheat must die before we have a harvest. The apple seed must die before we have an apple.

Likewise, your desire is a gift of God. Therefore, God does not mock you. You say, "God, Who gave me this desire, reveals the perfect plan for its development." And you contemplate the end. Faith is your attitude of mind. Faith is your thought. Whatever you impress in your subconscious is expressed on the screen of space. Nowhere in any holy book in the world does it say you have to have faith in Catholicism, Buddhism, Judaism, Hinduism, Shintoism, or any "ism." You have faith in the creative laws of your own mind. You have faith in the goodness of God in the land of the living. You have faith that there is an Infinite Intelligence that responds to your thought. It will respond to an atheist, agnostic—anybody. And before you call, the answer is there. It was always there.

Faith is your attitude of mind. It's what you expect, what you are focused on. The things that you are vividly imagining will come to pass. Some people are afraid of old age. Age is not the flight of years; it's the dawn of wisdom. Some are afraid of death. There is no reason to fear death. Death is simply a new birth; that's all that is. You go to sleep every night. That's where you go when you are called dead. In their ignorance they say that. People are afraid of the things that do not exist. You are alive, and your life is God's life. You are alive now. God is life eternal. Because God lives, you live. God cannot die; therefore, you cannot die.

Realize God is your employer, and the God Presence is always taking care of you. The great dancer says, "I dance for Him." The great singer says, "God sings in majestic cadences through me." He commands that internal power and wisdom. He calls upon it and it answers him. Naturally, he gets honors. He gets emoluments. He gets the praise of other people, but he doesn't seek it. He turns to the Source, and all these things are added to him.

Seek ye first the kingdom of God, and all these things, like honors, wealth, and everything else, will be added to you automatically. You will never want for anything. When someone makes a negative statement about you, begin to dwell on the fact that "I will fear no evil, for Thou art with me. Thy rod and Thy staff, they comfort me. Perfect love casteth out fear, for fear hath a torment. He that feareth is not made perfect in love."

Fearful people are always very selfish. They are wrapped up in themselves. They are hugging the shore. Love is always outgoing. It is an emanation. Fear is turning within in morbid introspection, believing someone is going to hurt you, that evil spirits can possess you. All this is ignorance. Ignorance is the only sin, and all the punishment is the consequence of that ignorance. Ignorance is the only devil in the world.

When you believe in external powers, you deny the One True Cause, which moves as a unity. It is the Life Principle within you, forever seeking to express itself as love, bliss, joy and right action. When we are fearful, we are selfish in the wrong way. Fear is a morbid introspection. Cease building a wall around yourself, saying, "I'm going to get hurt." Realize God is, and all that exists is God. Realize the love of God surrounds you, unfolds, and enwraps you. Say to yourself, "God walks and talks in me. I know I am one with my Father, and my Father is God. I have faith in God; therefore, I fear not." Fear not, little flock, for it is your Father's good pleasure to give you the kingdom.

Realize that you are surrounded by Divine love. That God's power is with your thoughts of good—that you are immersed in the Holy Omnipresence. God be with you.

The fear of the Lord is the beginning of wisdom. When you learn the laws of electricity, you are very careful how you apply them, because you know the consequences. You know that if you put your hand on a naked wire or cause a short circuit, what will happen. You learn the theories about insulation, conductivity, resulting in a healthy respect and reverence for these laws. And you will follow the nature of the principles.

Likewise, when you learn the principle of chemistry, you have a very healthy respect for the combination of chemicals, their atomic weight, because you know the disastrous consequences of mixing things together when you do not know the results. For instance, if you mix nitric acid and glycerin, you will have a powerful explosive.

Fear is a reverence, a healthy respect. You have a healthy respect for the law of your mind when you learn the consequences of misusing it, because your mind is a principle. Nothing can give you peace but the triumph of principles, Emerson said. You have a healthy respect for the fire, so you don't put your finger into it.

Similarly, when you know that your mind is a principle, like the principles of chemistry and physics, you will have a very healthy respect for the subconscious mind. A principle doesn't change. God is the Living Spirit within you. It's Infinite Intelligence, Boundless Wisdom. It's the Only Cause, Power, and Substance in the world. It's Supreme and Omnipotent. There is nothing to oppose it, nothing to challenge it, nothing to vitiate it. If there were two powers, there would be two wills. There would be chaos everywhere. There would be no order, symmetry, or proportion anywhere.

When you think God's thoughts, God's power is with your thoughts of good. You can tune in on the Infinite. The only immaterial power you know is your thought. In the beginning was the word. The word was with God, and the word was God. The word is a thought expressed. When you have discovered the power of your thoughts you have discovered God in that sense; because your thought is creative, not because it is *your* thought, but because it is thought. You can demonstrate that, of course, under hypnosis.

You can put a finger on a person's neck and say, "This is a red hot poker." That person will get a blister. You know very well that your thoughts become flesh, become manifest in your life. And you'd better have a healthy respect for your thoughts.

Water runs down hill. It expands when frozen. Takes the shape of any vessel into which it is poured. These and many other characteristics determine the principle by which water operates. We learn that it runs down hill. Your mind operates in the same way. If you think good, good follows; if you think evil, evil follows. Evil is the misuse of the law, misinterpretation of life. There is only One Power: That's the Living Spirit Almighty, which is undifferentiated, undefined, which is the Self-Originating Spirit.

Your mind is creative. That is, the thought in your mind is creative. Therefore, if you think good, good follows; if you think evil, evil follows. If you say, "The Infinite Healing Presence can heal me now," It will respond to you. You can say, "Infinite Intelligence guides and directs me, watches over me in all my ways." Faith is an attitude of mind. Faith is the use you make of your mind. Therefore, realize that fear is a thought in your own mind created by yourself. It has no reality; it's a shadow in your mind. The thing you are afraid of does not exist. Fear is faith in the wrong thing. Fear is faith upside down. Fear is God upside down. It's a twisted, morbid concept of life.

Fear has the same physiological effect as if it were real. Just the same as if a boy were in a chair and you told him a bogeyman was downstairs with a black bag and was going to take him away because he was a bad boy. He's frozen to the chair. He gets white and rigid. Yet, there is no reality to the thought. Take him downstairs and point out to him there is no bogeyman; he is free of the fear. But it had the same physiological and physical effect as if it were real.

Basil King, who wrote *The Conquest of Fear*, says that he was going blind. He was a young man, depressed, dejected, and feared the future, blindness and old age. He said he recalled something that a teacher said years ago. The Life Principle (God) in you is indestructible, invulnerable, and eternal. It always brings about the expedient, which is an answer to the particular need of any person. He used to think that Nature was cruel and raw and that evil abounded in the world. He had strange concepts of God.

I might say that good and evil are the movements of your own mind relative to the One Being that is forever whole, pure and immaculate in itself.

It's the use that you make of the power. How do you use electricity? You can use it to kill a person or fry an egg. How do use nitric acid? Well, you can use it to blind a person, or you can paint a Madonna on a windowpane. You can use water to drown a child or quench his thirst. Surely, these things are not evil. The forces of nature are not evil. The Living Spirit is the God Presence in you. How are you using it?

This man who was going blind said he used to think that Nature was cruel and raw and that God was punishing him, and so on. Then he began to think the Life Principle within him had overcome every obstacle in the world, whether it was a flood, volcanic eruption, war and destruction of all kinds. The Life Principle goes on, invulnerable and eternal. You can't destroy life; life just is. You are alive. Your life is God.

The Life Principle gives fur to the animals in the north; it gives them hair in the Temperate Zone, It covers others with shells to preserve them. Others are given a poisonous fluid that they emit when attacked. It takes care of all forms of life, such as those that came out of the sea. It gave them legs, made them stand upright; gave them wings to fly in the air. Always the Life Principle met the particular need.

When our ancient ancestors met the tiger, they were frozen with fear. Gradually, there came to their aid the dawn of reason, imagination and memory. There was a time when humans had no memory. Later, they began to think; and this Power within them responded to their thoughts.

Basil King, in meditating and musing on the Power within him, discovered that the natural principle, or life, or nature, is not cruel; but when he combined or united with this Principle in thought, mighty forces came to his aid. He no longer believed in three old men sitting on a throne, Father, Son, and Holy Ghost. But he perceived that God was the Life Principle. The Trinity is your Spirit, mind and body; or Spirit, mind and function because you need a body to express. And the mind is the priest, or the intermediary, between the Invisible and the visible; namely, your own thought. Therefore, the Spirit responds to the nature of your thought.

The average person has pigeonholed this God Presence and brings Him out on the sabbath, holidays, and cases of death, birth and marriage. But the rest of the time, the God Presence is put away in a corner. Some people are afraid to use the term *God*. Others look askance when God is mentioned, as they begin to think of God in terms of religious connotations because each has a different concept of God. God is your mind, your Spirit. God is your thought, too. Because your thought is creative, you have a healthy respect for It. Think of harmony, peace, love, right action and beauty. Think of an Infinite Healing Presence. Think that the sacred circle of God's Eternal Love surrounds you.

Think of a circle. Imagine you are in the midst of the circle. That's a circle of love, peace, harmony and power. Then nothing will touch you. You are immunized. You are God-intoxicated. You are always in the sacred center of God's Eternal Love.

Basil King discarded all the sentimental connotations associated with the name of Deity. He began to realize that God was the Life Principle within him, the Spirit, the mind, operating through him. When he united with this Infinite Intelligence, mighty forces came to his aid. He found this Creative Intelligence was the answer to every problem. He said, "This realization was the beginning of the process of casting out fear, which was blinding me and paralyzing me."

You cannot conquer fear until you come back to the fact that there is only One Power, One Presence, One Cause, One Substance. Therefore, you'd better get it straight in your cranium that the minute you give attention to externals, you are denying the One Presence and the One Power. A scientific thinker does not make a created thing greater than the Creator, therefore, get it clear and straight in your mind that never again will you give power to any person, place or thing, condition or circumstance, star, sun, moon, weather, water, or anything in this universe to harm, hurt or bless you. You simply recognize there is only One Creative Power: that is the Spirit and the mind in you. It's Almighty, Over All, Through All, and In All. It's the Only Cause. It's Supreme and Omnipotent. There is nothing to oppose it.

Will you tell me, what can oppose Omnipotence? Is there something? Produce it. Show it to me. Let me look at it. It has no reality. It's a shadow in your mind. Fear is a conglomeration of sinister shadows. You are fighting a shadow in your mind. You are the creator of your own fears. These fears have no reality.

Come back, therefore, to the One Presence and the One Power. When you reject and refuse to believe that any person, place or thing, condition or circumstance can hurt or harm you, then you are on the way. That's your great rejection. Then comes the great affirmation:

"I am God and there is no God beside me. From the rising of the sun to the setting of the same, there is none else. I am the Lord, thy God. My glory you shall not give to another, neither shall you give my praise. I am the Lord, thy God, that brought thee out of the land of Egypt, out of the house of bondage. There is no other God before me. I am, and there is none else.

And the Lord is my light and my salvation. Whom shall I fear?

The Lord is the strength of my life; of whom shall I be afraid? For in time of trouble He will hide me in His pavillion. In the secret of His tabernacle he shall hide me. He shall set me up upon a rock—the rock of truth—the same yesterday, today and forever."

Are you standing on that rock? It's All Powerful, All Wise, the Ever-Living One, the All Wise One, the All Knowing One. You are the Trinity yourself. You are the triangle, and you are the circle. The triangle is the Spirit, mind and body; Spirit, mind and function. You are this being. There is only One Power, One Presence, and Its Source is Love. It has no opposition. It is the Life Principle. It has overcome every opposition in this world and goes on conquering and to conquer. There is nothing to oppose it. It is Omnipotent.

Thoreau wrote that we are born to succeed, not to fail. You were born to win. How could the Infinite within you fail? Meditate on this.

Do not look for flattery from others. Do not look to others for promotion or aggrandizement. Turn within and realize that you promote yourself. That success is yours, harmony is yours, right action is yours, and beauty is yours. And when you establish the mental equivalent in your mind, there is no person, place, thing, or any power in the world that can prevent you from promotion, recognition, expression, achieving your goal, for the Infinite cannot fail. You are a Spiritual being. You are one with the Infinite. The Infinite cannot fail. You don't want dominion over other people. You want dominion over your own thoughts, feelings, actions and reactions. And you want that now.

Many have faith in evil powers that will bring harm to them. Others have faith in a hell, a lake of fire waiting for them. All of this, of course, is utter nonsense. Faith is an attitude, an expectancy. Some expect to be passed over for promotion. Whatever you deeply expect, of course, you will experience. How can you believe in a good future if you fear death and torment? You cannot. There is only one power.

"God is all in all, in all, over all, through all, and all in all. Omnipresent. Present everywhere." He said, "If that's so (which it is), there is no room for anyone else, is there?"

Do not think that God is cruel and He is punishing you, that God has created a hell for you because you have erred, when you couldn't help yourself anyway All humans have to err, because that's the only way we are going to grow, expand. It is impossible for anybody to banish fear if you have been indoctrinated in a fear of the future and after-life—if you have been taught that God is a God of fear. But God is a God of love.

In order to banish abnormal fear, you have to come back to the fundamental truth that there is but One Power. The Lord, thy God, is One Lord, One Power. Not two or three, or a thousand. Just one. It moves as unity. It is all love, all peace, all harmony. Align yourself with that and all fear will go away.

When we are fearful or indulge in negative thoughts, we are vibrating at a low level. When we meditate on the Psalms and say, "The Lord is my shepherd; I shall not want," or "The Presence of God is right here where I am," or "I dwell in the secret place of the Most High and God is guiding me now," we are thinking spiritually. We are vibrating at a higher level at a spiritual frequency. And just as when we place a finger on the tuning fork, it is the end of the negative vibration. This is the end of the evil, because evil is a false belief about God and the Infinite Goodness of the One Who Forever Is.

You have the capacity to easily destroy, neutralize fear by simply changing the thought. Fear depresses, suppresses, strangles. If it were indulged in, it will change a positive, creative mental attitude into a non-productive, negative one, and this is fatal to achievement. The effect of fear, especially where the fear thought has become habitual, is to dry up the very source of life. Faith that replaces fear has just the opposite effect upon the body and brain. It enlarges, opens up the nature, gives abundant life to the cells and increases the brainpower.

Fear works terrible havoc with the imagination, which pictures all sorts of dire things. Faith is its perfect antidote, for, while fear sees only the darkness and the shadows, faith sees the silver lining, the sun behind the cloud. Fear looks down, and expects the worst; faith looks up and anticipates the best. Fear is pessimistic; faith is optimistic. Fear always predicts failure; faith predicts success. There can be no fear of poverty or failure when the mind is dominated by faith. Doubt cannot exist in its presence. It is above all adversity.

A powerful faith is a great life-prolonger, because it never frets; it sees beyond the temporary annoyance, the discord, the trouble, it sees the sun behind the cloud. It knows things will come out right, because it sees the goal that the eye cannot see.

You can cast out fear. You can affirm boldly by repeating:

"I have absolute trust in the God Presence within me. I expect the best. I know only good can come to me. Divine love in me casts out fear. I am at peace. I see the Presence of God everywhere. I am absolutely fearless. God, or the Divine Presence, is with me always. It made me, created me, sustains me. It's the Invisible Life Principle within me. It loves me and cares for me, for it is written: 'He cares for me.' If God be for me, who can be against me? I know that one with God is a majority. This heals and frees me from all sense of fear. Only God's thoughts come to me. These thoughts continually unfold, bringing me harmony, joy, peace and success. I am surrounded by Divine love. I think rightly on all occasions. God's Power is with my thoughts of good. The love, the life and the truth of God flow through me now. I am immersed in the Holy Omnipresence. The Infinite ocean of peace always surrounds me. I am full of Divine understanding. Divine love goes before me, today and every day, to make straight, perfect and joyous my way."

In this meditation, you are sending the messengers of peace, love, harmony, right action and beauty into your subconscious mind. And these messengers fulfill your orders. They are faithful messengers. You will discover that all your ways are pleasantness and all your paths are peace.

You are one with your Father within, and your Father is God. Fear not, He said, little flock, for it is your Father's good pleasure to give you the kingdom. And that kingdom of god is within you. The love, the light and the glory of God surrounds you, enfolds you and enwraps you. The Divine Presence governs you now. You love to work with others. You love to represent and express God's ideas.

So, affirm boldly:

God's ideas unfold within me bringing me harmony, health, peace and joy. I will fear no evil for Thou art with me. Thy rod and Thy staff they comfort me. I know goodness and mercy follows me all the days of my life, for I dwell in the house of God forever. I dwell in the secret place of the Most High. I abide in the shadow of the Almighty. I will say of the Lord: He is my refuge, my fortress, my God; in Him will I trust. He covers me with His feathers and under His wing shall I rest. The truth of God is my shield and buckler. His angels watch over me. They bear me up lest I dash my foot against a stone, for God is love and He cares for me.

In a Nutshell

Fear is like a poison gas pumped into one's atmosphere,
It causes mental, moral, and spiritual asphyxiation, and
sometimes death—death to energy, death to tissue, and
death to all growth

Fear and worry make us attract the very things we
dread. The fear habit impairs health, shortens life and paralyzes efficiency. Doubt and fear mean failure; faith is an
optimist, fear a pessimist.

Do not let yourself be subservient to another's thoughts.
Have a healthy, reverent respect for your thought, because
your thought is your prayer. What you feel, you attract;
what you imagine, you become.

Your thought governs you, not another. Stand tall.
Stand up straight, and say: "I am one with the Infinite,
which lies stretched in smiling repose."

Fearful people are always very selfish. They are
wrapped up in themselves. Love is always outgoing. It is an
emanation. Fear is turning within in morbid introspection,
believing someone is going to hurt you, that evil spirits can
possess you. All this is ignorance. Ignorance is the only sin,
and all the punishment is the consequence of that ignorance. Ignorance is the only devil in the world.

Realize that fear is a thought in your own mind created
by yourself. It has no reality; it's a shadow in your mind.
The thing you are afraid of does not exist. Fear is faith in

the wrong thing. Fear is faith upside down. Fear is God upside down. It's a twisted, morbid concept of life.

God is the Life Principle. The Trinity is your Spirit, mind and body; or Spirit, mind and function because you need a body to express. And the mind is the priest, or the intermediary, between the Invisible and the visible; namely, your own thought. Therefore, the Spirit responds to the nature of your thoughts.

All humans have to err, because that's the only way we are going to grow, and expand, It is impossible for anybody to banish fear if you have been indoctrinated in a fear of the future and afterlife—if you have been taught that God is a God of fear. But God is a God of love.

In order to banish abnormal fear, you have to come back to the fundamental truth that there is but One Power. The Lord, thy God, is One Lord, One Power. Not two or three, or a thousand. Just one. It moves as unity. It is all love, all peace, and all harmony. Align yourself with that and all fear will go away.

CHAPTER FOUR

The Healing Power of Love

There is only one love. It is pure, perfect, undefiled, approving, abundant and generous. It never changes nor wavers nor weakens. It is God. We love because God first loved us. God is the source of love. Love frees, gives; it is the Spirit of God. You practice love when you have an emanation of goodwill. It's an outreaching of the heart, wishing for every person what you wish for yourself. You can wish for everyone health, happiness, peace, and all the blessings of life. As you do this, you are also doing it to yourself, because you are thinking it and feeling it. Whatever you think and feel you create in your own life, in your own body, in your own circumstances. This One Power has no opposition. It is the Omnipotent Life Principle that has overcome every opposition in this world. It goes on conquering and to conquer. It is forever victorious.

This is the basic truth of every religion of the world during all the ages of time. The heightened expansive awareness of this essential nature of a supreme, intelligent and loving Presence has been expressed and iterated by every inspired leader of whom we have knowledge. All have insisted that just as the sun shines equally on the rich and the poor, the strong and the weak, the intelligent and the ignorant, those who are holy and those who are evil, God's absolute love shines on and is radiant within all people.

No one is excluded from the love of God nor is anyone forgotten, neglected or lost in Divine love. It is omnipresent, omniscient, and all-inclusive. Everybody who begins to live in the conscious awareness of absolute and holy love will experience a definite response of divine love within— no matter where, when or what is taking place around them—no matter who they are.

God's love responds to everyone as a liberating, lightening of the heart. It is a higher awareness of consciousness, which heals and makes us whole again.

You must have a healthy, reverent, wholesome respect for the Divinity within you, which shapes your ends. The bible tells us: "Love thy neighbor as thyself." By neighbor it means the closest thing to you, which is the Living Spirit Almighty—closer than breathing, nearer than hands and feet.

Love in the Bible is loyalty, recognition, giving all your loyalty, devotion, and recognition to the Divine

Presence within you. Emerson said, "I, the imperfect, adore the Perfect." So put it first in your life. Then you will automatically respect the Divinity in others. But if you don't love the God Self within you, honor it and exalt it, you can't salute the Divinity in any person. You can't honor the Divinity in another if you don't honor it in yourself. How could you? That's the "Love thy neighbor as thyself," for the self of you is the neighbor, the closest thing to you.

This is not egotism, egoism, self-aggrandizement or narcissism. Not at all. It's having a healthy reverence for the God Presence within you, which created you and the whole world. Surely, if you don't honor and exalt that, how can you honor it and exalt it in your wife, husband, son, daughter, or anybody?

Some people are unsure what is meant by "love" in the Bible and other religious writings. We are taught to "love" everyone—good and bad alike. "Love" here means to see the presence of God everywhere, present in everything, the life energy of humankind—saint and sinner alike.

Let's reconsider the intent of the word *love* and lift our minds above what the world generally considers love to be to divine love. The pure essence of being that joins and binds in harmony the universe and everything in it. It is the greatest harmonizing principle we know. It is the universal solvent. It is a love that shines on the just and the unjust, divine love loves for the sake and joy of loving.

Love in divine sense is an act of compassion and mercy and our every attempt to practice divine love is effective at some time, in a certain way. Granted, we are not perfect, but we can and are able and should become committed to practicing and living according to the golden rule and the law of love.

Murray L. was a successful business executive. He was respected and admired by his employees, his customers and in his community. He came to me one day, very upset. "I have been chosen by our Chamber of Commerce as 'Man of the Year.' It is a great honor, but I have to give a speech at the presentation. I am absolutely terrified when it comes to public speaking. What can I do?"

I suggested that he go into a quite place three or four times a day where he would not be disturbed. He should sit comfortably in an armchair; relax his body to the utmost. This physical inertia will render his mind more receptive to his affirmations. Then say the following aloud:

I am completely relaxed and at ease. I am poised, serene, and calm. At the presentation I will make a fine speech, I will be calm and collected. I will present my message clearly and with confidence. The audience will be friendly and receptive and enjoy my speech. I will do this because God is within me and He gives me the strength and courage I need. My message is God's message. My speech is God speaking through me. The audience congratulates me. I am at peace in my mind.

Murray did this each day prior to the presentation. When he stood on the dais facing his audience, he was confident and at ease. He spoke flawlessly and was given a standing ovation.

When you mentally and emotionally unite with honesty, integrity, justice, goodwill and happiness, you love God, because you love that which is good. You are loving God when you are fascinated, absorbed and captivated by the great truth that God is One and Indivisible, and there are no divisions or quarrels in It. To love God is to give your allegiance, devotion and loyalty to the One Power, refusing to recognize any other power in the world. When you definitely recognize and completely accept in your mind that God really is Omnipotent in the most practical, literal and most matter of fact manner, you are loving God, because you are loyal to the One Power.

Sit down quietly at times and think over this vital, interesting, fascinating and greatest of all truths: that God is the only Power, that everything we can become aware of is part of His self-expression.

A young mother approached me after one of my lectures. She told me how afraid she was of hurting her children. She said, "I have a very bad temper. I am easily upset and even when my children do trivial things that annoy me, I scream at them and sometimes hit them. The poor kids are afraid of me and I'm afraid that someday I will really hurt them."

I told her: You must cleanse your subconscious mind of anger. It is not easy, but you must replace the anger that may have been inculcated in your mind when you were a child by parents or teachers or others in authority. Several times a day, when the children are at school or away, go to a quiet place and repeat the following mediation:

God's love fills my soul. God is with me now. Free me from the thoughts of anger that have permeated my mind. My children are good. They want to be loved not punished. Divine love flows through me to them. God's love for me will help me control my temper and will sink deep into my subconscious mind so that my actions will reflect this love.

It did not take long. God's Power captivated her imagination. It filled her through and through. She became entranced with the idea of being a good mother. This love caused her to persist in her efforts to control her anger. This, truly, is love. Soon the feelings of anger went away. Anger was swallowed up in love, because love and anger cannot dwell together.

The Bible says: "By this shall all know that you are my disciples: If you love one another." God is absolute love. Hence, it follows that before the appeal is made, the answer is given. The love of God flows through you now. You are surrounded by the peace of God. All is well.

Affirm boldly:

Divine love surrounds me, enfolds me, and encompasses me. This Infinite love is inscribed in my heart and written on my inward parts. I radiate love in thought, words and deeds. Love unifies and harmonizes all the powers, attributes and qualities of God within me.

Love means joy, peace, freedom, bliss and praise. Love is freedom. It opens prison doors, and sets free all the captives.

Everyone represents Divine love in operation. I salute the Divinity in the other. I know and believe that Divine love heals me now. Love is the guiding principle in me. It brings into my experience perfect, harmonious relationships. God is love, and those that dwell in love dwell in God, and God in them. You must believe that the love, the light and the glory of God surrounds you, enfolds you and enwraps you. And into whatsoever house you enter, first say, "Peace be to this house."

Affirm boldly:

My mind is flooded with the life, the love and the truth of God. Whenever my attention wanders away, I bring it back to the contemplation of His Divine Presence. I enter into the secret chamber within myself. It's my own mind where I walk and talk with the Infinite. I am in the heavens of my own mind because I am at peace. I am perfectly quiet, calm, serene and poised. Peace be within thy walls and prosperity within thy palaces. For my brethren and companions' sake, I will say, "Peace be within thee."

I live in the house of the Lord, my God. I seek only the good. I am living in His kingdom. I feel and sense the Divine atmosphere of peace, love and joy. I stir up the gift of God within me. I know that I and my Father are one. I sense and feel the reality of this. His life flows through me now. I know that in this heaven where I live, move and have my being all my prayers are answered. I am at peace. The dove of love has whispered in my ear, 'Peace be still.' For God is the Only Presence, and the Only Power, and the Only Presence here now. And all the rest is but shadow. In Him we live, move and have our being. God's love, life and truth move in me now.

Fear thoughts, worry thoughts, negative thoughts of any kind will not hurt you unless you entertain them for a long period of time and emotionalize them deeply. Otherwise, they will not hurt you in the slightest. They are potential trouble for you, but as yet, they are not actualized. Your fears cannot be actualized unless you emotionalize them, thereby impressing your subconscious mind. Whatever is impressed on the subconscious mind is impressed and expressed on the screen of space. So into whatsoever house ye enter, first say, "Peace be to this house." For God is love, and those that dwell in love dwell in God and God in them.

You are dwelling in the secret place of the Most High, because your mind is a secret place. No one knows what you are thinking or planning. You are thinking on whatsoever things are true, whatsoever things are lovely, whatsoever things are just, and whatsoever things are pure, and whatsoever things are of good report. If there be any virtue, if there be any praise, think on these things. For you are what you think all day long. For as you think in your heart, so you are, so do you experience, so do you become. Under His wings I shall trust. His truth is your shield and buckler.

=========== **In a Nutshell** ===========

There is only one love. It is pure, perfect, undefiled, approving, abundant and generous. It never changes nor wavers nor weakens. It is God. We love because God first loved us. God is the source of love.

God's love responds to everyone as a liberating, lightening of the heart. It is a higher awareness of consciousness, which heals and makes us whole again.

Love in divine sense is an act of compassion and mercy and our every attempt to practice divine love is effective at some time, in a certain way. Granted, we are not perfect, but we can and are able and should become committed to practicing and living according to the golden rule and the law of love.

To love God is to give your allegiance, devotion and loyalty to the One Power, refusing to recognize any other power in the world. When you definitely recognize and completely accept in your mind that God really is Omnipotent in the most practical, literal and most matter of fact manner, you are loving God, because you are loyal to the One Power.

Faith is an attitude of mind. It's a way of thinking. You have faith if you have a mental image of accomplishing something wonderful, and if you sustain it with expectancy and confidence, your subconscious mind will bring that to pass.

If you want to conquer fear, you have to come back to the truth that there is only One Power, Indivisible, and a Source of love. When you know that, when you align with it, you can't be fearful, you can't worry. This Power has no opposition. There is nothing to oppose it, challenge it, vitiate it or thwart it. It is the Life Principle. It has overcome every opposition in the world. It's Omnipotent, All Powerful, goes on conquering and to conquer.

The love, the light and the glory of God surrounds you, enfolds you and enwraps you. The Divine Presence governs you now. You love to work with others. You love to represent and express God's ideas. So, affirm boldly: "God's ideas unfold within me bringing me harmony, health, peace and joy."

CHAPTER FIVE

The Inner Meaning of The 23rd Psalm

The Lord is my shepherd; I shall not want.
He maketh me to lie down in green pastures:
he leadeth me beside the still waters.
He restoreth my soul: he leadeth me in the paths of
righteousness for his name's sake.
Yea, though I walk through the valley of the shadow
of death, I will fear no evil: for thou art with me;
thy rod and thy staff they comfort me.
Thou preparest a table before me in the presence of
mine enemies: thou anointest my head with oil;
my cup runneth over.
Surely goodness and mercy shall follow me all the
days of my life: and I will dwell in the house of
the Lord for ever.

his is the 23rd Psalm. This is probably the most frequently repeated psalm from the Judeo-Christian bible. Many people of all faiths meditate on the great truths of this Psalm. They get marvelous results. As you focus your attention on these truths, absorbing them into your mentality, you are meditating in the true sense of the word; because you are appropriating more of your Divinity, the Divine Presence that dwells in the deep-cell of all people.

Meditation determines your destiny. We are always meditating. Your thoughts and feelings control your destiny. Meditation is as real and as natural as digestion, assimilation, and breathing.

In Las Vegas I met a woman who suffered from shock. She had lost her voice. The doctors could find no infection, no affliction of any kind in examining the throat and the vocal organs. At my suggestion, she began to practice what I call *real meditation*. Her son was coming home from Vietnam in a few weeks, and she sat still and quiet and imagined that she was embracing him and welcoming him home, saying all the things a mother would say. She did this for about ten minutes two or three times a day. She gave attention to a selected goal, an objective. At the end of two weeks her son came home, knocked at the door, and she welcomed him. She began to talk naturally. That's real meditation. She gave attention to her voice. She gave attention to the fact that she was talking, to the fact that she was welcoming him. It was a mental and spiritual drama taking place in her own mind.

The Lord is my shepherd. The *Lord* means God, the Living Spirit Almighty, in particular your awareness and knowledge of this Infinite Presence and Power within you. The shepherd takes care of the sheep, and the Divine Power will take care of you. As you turn to this Indwelling Presence, Its nature is to respond to you.

You are told: *I shall not want.* This means you will never want for evidence of the fact that you have chosen God as your shepherd. Shepherds watch over their sheep. They love them and care for them. They examine the field where they graze and eradicate locoweed, which would adversely affect the sheep. They lead them to the shade and guide them single file over the steep ravine to water, where they are refreshed. At night they examine their nostrils to see if there are any other needles or other irritants embedded therein. If so, they pluck them out and pour some soothing oil upon them. They examine their feet, also; and, if injured, they administer kindly to them with whatever medication or treatment is appropriate.

Shepherds love their sheep. All this is symbolic, of course, and very significant, indicating to all of us that if we choose God as our shepherd, and God is the Living Spirit within you, the Supreme Intelligence, the Life Principle. We will not want for any good thing if we choose the Supreme Intelligence as our guide and counselor.

Before we get an answer to our prayer, we must first possess our desire in consciousness. We must establish the mental equivalent. We do this by thinking of what we want with interest and feeling, and give it our attention. Gradually, by osmosis, it sinks into our subconscious mind and becomes a conviction.

Our consciousness represents the sum total of our acceptances and beliefs, both conscious and subconscious. Our state of consciousness is the way we think, feel, and believe, and to whatever we give mental consent. That's the Only Presence, Power, Cause, and Substance in your world. When you discover that, you have discovered God within you. In other words, our desire must be deposited in our subconscious mind. We must be before we can have.

The ancient Hebrews said "to be is to have." If I try to obtain what I want by external means, the Bible tells you, I am a thief and a robber. My state of consciousness is the door to all expression. That's the way you think, feel, and believe. It is done unto you, as you believe, the way you believe. I must possess the mental equivalent of whatever I want to be or possess in this world.

Let us take a simple illustration. You want to be healed and you affirm over and over again, "I am healed." These mechanical statements are not enough. You must enter into the joy of feeling that you are healed. You must realize there is an Infinite Healing Presence Which created you from a cell. It knows all the processes and functions of your body. It heals a cut in your finger, reduces the edema of a burn, It restores you. The tendency of all life is to heal. It must be a conviction based upon the silent inner knowing of the soul.

To be wealthy, you must assume the *feeling* of being wealthy and realize that God, or Spirit within you, is the Source of the entire world, the Source of the hair on your head, the Source of the bread on your table, the shoes that you wear, the ground you walk on, the air that you breathe, the Source of the sunshine, and the Source of the stars that come nightly to the sky. Then wealth will follow based upon your knowledge, awareness, feeling, and understanding.

The sheep are the noble, dignified, God-like ideas that bless us. Our conviction of good is the shepherd that watches over the sheep. Our dominant state of mind always rules in the same manner as a general commands the army. We call our sheep by name when we enter into the consciousness of them having, being, or doing the thing we long to have, to be, or to do. If we sustain these moods, they gel and crystallize within us; and these subjective embodiments become objectified manifestations.

The sheep will not follow strangers, but will flee from them; for they do not know the voice of strangers. The strangers are the thoughts of fear, doubt, condemnation, jealousy, envy, or anxiety that enter the mind. These ideas delay our healing or prosperity and postpone our demonstration; because these thoughts are the voice of strangers.

For example, if there were 20,000 sheep in a corral and there were ten shepherds, and they came in the morning to lead the sheep out, they would say, "Follow me." All the sheep of that shepherd knew his voice, and they would follow him. But if a stranger said, "Follow me," there would be no response. This simply means, when you have the mood or the feeling of being what you long to be and you know there is an Almighty Power backing you up, moving in your behalf, then that ideal that you want to bring to pass will come to pass and the light will shine upon your ways.

It is idle to pray that the Infinite Healing Presence is making you whole and perfect and at the same time be resentful or fearful that you cannot be healed. If you believe that circumstances, conditions, age, events, race, lack of money, can preclude the possibility of attaining your objective, you are in Biblical language a thief and a robber, because you are robbing yourself of the joy of the answered prayer. There is nothing to oppose the Infinite, and the Infinite Spirit gave you the desire. The desire is good; therefore, you say that Infinite Spirit gave you this desire. It doesn't mock me. It will reveal the perfect plan for its development in Divine law and order.

The seed you deposit in the ground has its own mathematics and mechanics in it. The oak is the realized potential of the acorn, but you must first deposit the acorn in the soil. And the seed is faith, because you understand the Divine law. And the seed is your desire, a new invention, a new book, or a desire to become greater than you are. All that ever came before me, the Bible says, the conviction are thieves and robbers. You must believe that you now are what you long to be. To believe is to live in the state of being it, to be alive to the truths. To accept something as true is belief. Millions believe that which is false.

Many people meditate. In India, for example, they give you a word to repeat over and over again, Doing this quiets the mind and concentrates your thoughts. Various people to accomplish this use Sanskrit Words like *Ohm*, *Ayim*, or *Sharim*. You may prefer to use a word more meaningful to you such as *insight*, *peace*, *love*, or *I am*. Any word or phrase will do, even a word like *Coca Cola*, if repeated over and over will help create a quiet mind. Your blood pressure will drop; your pulse will become normal and all that. But such words will not help you grow in a spiritual way. You could grow spiritually by repeating, "Divine love fills my soul," or "God's peace fills my mind." You must know what you are doing. To say an idle word and not know the meaning of it doesn't accomplish very much.

Meditation comes from "med," which means the middle, the medium between the idea and its manifestation. Medicus is an old term for doctor, because doctors were looked upon as the medium between the disease and health. Everybody meditates. Some people meditate on negative things such as financial losses, the blowout on the lonely road, ill health or bad decisions they had made That is meditation of a very negative nature and; because you are giving those thoughts your full attention and devotion, they sink into your subconscious mind and, you magnify them, and you bring all these things to pass in your own life.

Meditate on whatsoever things are true, lovely, noble, and God-like. To meditate is to eat all these truths, to cogitate, to give your attention to something, to focus on something. They asked Newton how he accomplished great things. He said, I intend my mind in a certain direction. In other words, he focused on a solution, the way out, the happy ending. To cogitate, to meditate, to focus your attention upon, to get interested in something, get absorbed in something.

You are told that meditation is for the purpose of redirecting your mind along God-like ways so that Divine law and order may govern all of your activities in all the phases of your life. There is nothing mysterious about meditation. You are always meditating—perhaps, not always constructively. Shakespeare said, "All things be ready if the mind be so." The Bible says the works were finished from the foundation of the world All this means is that we should open our minds and hearts and accept the gifts of God proffered to us from the foundations of time. Surely, you don't pray for sunshine, or air, or water. The ocean doesn't care whether you go to it with a thimble full or a demijohn, or a barrel. There is always the same amount of water in the world.

We should reorder our minds and ask ourselves the simple question: *How is it in God and heaven?* Heaven is that Infinite Intelligence in which you live, and move, and have your being. God is Spirit, and that Spirit is in you. The answer to that is: All is bliss, harmony, joy, love, peace, perfection, and all this indescribable beauty.

That's the reality of you, the All Wise One, the All Powerful One, the All Knowing One within you. No matter what you seek already is. Why wait for love? God's love is within you. Say that. Say, "God's love fills my soul." Peace is. You don't wait for it, do you? God's peace fills my soul.

The joy of the Lord is your strength. Power *is*. The Almighty Power *is* within you; it's timeless and spaceless. Harmony *is*. God is Absolute Harmony. The harmony of God is in your mind, in your body. The answer to every problem is within you now. For God is the timeless, spaceless Being within you, that Living Spirit Almighty.

It only knows the answer. No matter what you seek, already is. Why wait for it? If you say, "Some day I'll be happy." The world won't give you happiness; you give it to yourself. If you are seeking guidance, affirm: "Infinite Intelligence knows the answer, the way out. Even before I ask, as I call on the Supreme Wisdom, I know its nature is to respond to me. I will clearly recognize the lead, the answer, when it comes. I know it comes clearly into my conscious, reasoning mind; and I recognize it instantaneously. It's impossible for me to miss it."

Having done this, dismiss it from your mind knowing that you turned your request over to the Infinite Intelligence in your subconscious; and inevitably the answer will come. You know when you have really turned it over, because your mind is at peace and you don't subsequently deny what you have already affirmed and decreed.

He maketh me to lie down in green pastures. I am writing this chapter in a book in Laguna Hills, California. A letter arrived in the mail yesterday from a woman in Hawaii telling me that she meditated on these words. "He maketh me to lie down in green pastures." For about a half an hour three times a day for a week, she focused all her attention on this promise of the Psalm. She began to look at it from all angles. Its inner meaning, and how it applied to her. She stated that in her meditative mood and on her reflection of these words, the phrase meant peace of mind, contentment, tranquility, abundance, and security.

The vision of a cow lying down in the field chewing the cud came clearly into her mind, symbolizing the meditative process of her own mind. In chewing the cud, the cow is absorbing, digesting, and transforming everything eaten into milk, tissue, bone, muscle, blood, and so forth. Likewise, she was digesting, ingesting, and absorbing these truths until they, too, became a part of her. So as the cow chews on the clover, it goes from one stomach to another, and then comes up again, into the mouth of the cow; and it chews it again and again to a fine consistency; and, lo and behold, we have milk.

That's meditation. The ancients said, "You can eat the cow because it chews the cud and divides the hoof. It's clean unto you." Dividing the hoof is getting a clear understanding of what the truths of God are, separating your mind from that which is false; knowing, therefore, what the truth is, then you absorb, digest, give your attention and devotion to these truths. Then you are chewing the cud, and these become a part of you like an apple becomes your blood stream. That's meditation. It's practical; it's down to earth.

This woman's finances were in bad shape. She was in danger of losing her lovely home. The mine in which she had invested a large part of her money suddenly collapsed. Her son was missing; no one could find him. As she continued to meditate, at the end of a week she received notice from an attorney that a large sum of money had been bequeathed to her by a distant relative on another island, the big island of Hawaii. This solved her financial problem, and she was able to make satisfactory arrangements with all concerned. Her son returned home. He had run away to Canada thinking there were greener pastures there. He was wiser on his return and established peace within him.

This was real meditation of a very constructive nature. She appropriated mentally these great truths, and they became a living part of her the same way that a banana, when eaten, or a piece of bread, becomes a part of your blood stream. She quietly devoted her mind to a certain passage of the Psalm and dwelled on the profundity of its meaning and its healing power. She decided to lie down mentally with these truths and experience all around harmony in her life.

He leadeth me beside the still waters. The shepherd in the Bible is a symbol of the guiding, healing, protective power of the Divine Presence within you. You are a good shepherd when you know and believe that God, or the Supreme Intelligence, is the only Presence and Power, Cause, and Substance within you. This is the Power that enables you to walk and lift a chair; it's an unseen Power. When this conviction is enthroned in your mind, you will be Divinely directed and blessed in countless ways because the nature of Infinite Intelligence is responsiveness. Call upon me, I will answer you; I'll be with you in trouble. I will set you on High because you have known my name.

Name means the nature, the way it responds to you. The still waters represent the mind full of peace, poise, serenity, and equanimity. You are contemplating the power, the wisdom, and the love of the Infinite. In doing so, you find yourself immersed in the Holy Omnipresence, bathed by the river of peace, joy, wholeness, and vitality.

When your mind is at peace, the answer comes. You meditate, you know, you can eat mentally. You can digest and absorb certain ideas. Peace is the power at the heart of God.

He restoreth my soul. When you choose God, or the Supreme Intelligence, as your shepherd, you will sing the songs of triumph; or, to put it in Emerson's words: Your mental attitude will be the soliloquy of the loving and beholding soul. For prayer is the contemplation of the truths of God from the highest standpoint. You are recognizing the Infinite Spirit within you, and you know there will be a response when you call upon It. It's impersonal, no respecter of persons. It responds to the atheist, the agnostic. It responds to everybody. Call upon it and it answers you. It's no respecter of persons. It knows nothing about Islam, Judaism, Christianity, Buddhism, Shintoism, or any specific creed.

God is no respecter of persons. Love belongs to all. The law is always impersonal. That applies to any law. Furthermore, you recognize the Power is one and indivisible. As you do this, you reject all fear and false beliefs of the world. Whatever fears, frustrations, false beliefs were deposited in your subconscious mind can be obliterated and expunged, because you are claiming boldly that the Infinite ocean of life, love, truth, and beauty are saturating your subconscious mind, cleansing, healing, and transforming your whole being into the Divine pattern of harmony, wholeness, and peace, It is somewhat similar to pouring distilled water into a bottle of dirty, filthy water. After a while, the moment comes when the last drop of dirty water is removed. That's called prayer, filling your mind with the truths of God, and you crowd out of your mind everything unlike God.

Once you acknowledge the supremacy of the Supreme Healing Power and the Creative Power of your own thought, you have the Lord as your shepherd, and you have restored your soul.

He leadeth me in the paths of righteousness for his name's sake. Go within. Close your eyes. Become still and quiet. And gently affirm that the wisdom of God anoints your intellect and is always a lamp unto your feet; it's always a light upon your path. Claim that Divine love goes before you making straight, happy, joyous, and prosperous your way. Look to the Infinite Presence at all times, and think, speak, act, and react from the standpoint of the Divine Center within you. Realize, know, feel, and claim that Infinite Spirit is your guide, your counselor, your boss, your senior partner; and that Divine right action governs you at all times.

Affirm boldly:

From now on, I think right, because I think from the standpoint of eternal verities and principles of life. I feel right. I do right. I act right. And everything I do is in accordance with the eternal principles of Divine law and order, heaven's first law. I know that the name of the Infinite means the nature of the Infinite, which refers to the fact that the God Presence is the Ever Living One, the All Powerful One, the All Knowing One, the Self-renewing One, the Boundless One. And He is omnipresent, omniscient, and is also the omniaction of the Infinite. You know that the Infinite and His love saturate your whole being; whatever you do will prosper.

Realize that the Infinite is within you. It's called the Ever Living One, the All Wise One, the All Knowing One, the Self-renewing One, the One alone who lives in the hearts of all people. It is older than night or day, younger than the babe newborn, brighter than light, darker than dark, beyond all things and creatures, yet fixed in the hearts of everyone. And from it the shining worlds flow forth. The whole world comes forth from the One Presence and One Power. It is you. You came forth from the Infinite, also. The whole world is a creation of the Infinite.

In the Upanishads, the mystic teachings of the Hindus, it says, "God thinks and worlds appear." The whole world, modern science says, is a thought of the One, the Beautiful, and the Good. The whole world is also mathematically ordered by a Supreme Intelligence, so scientists can tell the return of the Halley's comet to a split second. It is a Divinely ordered universe, so that the astronauts, before they left the earth, could calculate mathematically that they could walk out in space. And, of course, they could. They had faith, not in a human or a corporeal personality, or a creed, or a dogma, or a church; not at all. They had faith in the Creative Laws of Mind, and principles that never change; it is the same yesterday, today, and forever.

Engineers have faith in the principles of mathematics. When they builds bridges, they conforms to universal principles of stress and strain, the curvature of the earth, and all these things. They calculate the whole thing mathematically. Navigators flying through the Pacific may not know where they are, but by shooting the stars they calculate the location, and latitude and longitude. Likewise, when you are lost or confused, you can shoot that great star within you, the I AM, the Presence of God, the Ohm of India. It's the Living Spirit Almighty. Contact that. It's All Wise. It created the whole world.

Realize Infinite Intelligence knows the answer, guides and directs you, and leads you, and reveals to you the answer, for It knows *only* the answer. This is why you read: Before you call, I will answer. Before you call, the answer is there, waiting for you, for the Infinite will do nothing for you except through you. The Infinite works on a cosmic scale, and you are an individual. You are free to choose; you have volition, choice, initiative. You have the freedom to become a cutthroat or a holy person. You are not compelled to be good, not compelled to be honest, not compelled to express love. You are not compelled to be successful, not like an animal governed by instinct. You have freedom of choice. You can choose from the kingdom of God within you. You can choose harmony. You can choose right action, which is the principle of life. You can choose beauty, love, inspiration, abundance, and security. You can choose from the Infinite Resources within you, from that Infinite Presence and Power Which is All Wise and knows all. You have volition and choice and initiative.

Your state of consciousness is the only God you'll ever know. Your state of consciousness is the way you think, feel, believe, and what you give mental consent to. There is no other Cause, or Power, or Substance in this world.

Therefore, if you are wise, you'll begin to believe in the goodness of God in the land of the living, in the guidance of God, the harmony of God, the love of God. And you realize that your sheep are the lovely, noble, God-like states you wish to embody. And they will follow you as you begin to feel that you now are what you long to be, that you are now doing what you love to do. If you are a singer, you now are the great singer; and God is singing in majestic cadences through you. As you continue, God in the midst of you will bring it to pass.

Yea, though I walk through the valley of the shadow of death, I will fear no evil: for thou art with me. And, of course, you know, thy rod and thy staff they comfort me. Wherever you go, walk the earth with the awareness of peace, love, and goodwill to all. Supposing you go into a hospital to see a sick friend and you are taking with you the mood of love, peace, and goodwill. Well, that's a wonderful way to visit a sick person. Your mental and spiritual atmosphere will bless the sick person. And when you pray for a sick person, never identify with symptoms, pains, aches, or corporeal conditions. Realize that the Presence of God is where the sick person is; and you realize the vitality, the wholeness, and the perfection of the Infinite are now being made manifest to the loved one. Then you see the loved one as the loved one ought to be. The person should be home; you don't see that person in the hospital, sick, wan, and weak. You are fastening that sickness on the person. You are also creating it in your own mind. It doesn't make any sense.

If you are praying for wholeness, vitality, and perfection, peace, and harmony, and for the miraculous Healing Power to flow through the person, Visualize that person home vital and alive. Your image must agree with your affirmation. This is why so many people do not know how to pray. This is why many do more harm than good. Because they are identifying with the sickness, condition, tumor, or whatever it might be. Or they look at the chart and say, "It's terrible; he hasn't got a chance," and so forth. That's no way to pray.

Your mental and spiritual atmosphere can bless the person if you have the right attitude. Give the person a transfusion of faith, confidence, trust, and love. Tell the person that the Miraculous Healing Power is within him or her, and give that person a transfusion of grace and love, power, and wisdom, thereby nourishing him or her with confidence and a belief in the Infinite Healing Presence. God is life; that is your life now. Do that whenever you visit a hospital or a sick person. Give that person a transfusion of life and love and beauty.

God is life, and that is your life now. Life cannot die; that would be absurd. So why talk about death? There is no death. It's a shadow. A shadow has no reality. How could life die, in other words? How could God die? God was never born, will never die; water wets it not, fire burns it not, wind blows it not away. It has no beginning or end. It's the Life Principle within you. How in the name of heaven could life become death? It's absurd! So-called death is an entry into the fourth dimension of life, and you go there every night when people in their gross ignorance call you dead. You go there every night in your life. That's where you go when you are called *dead*. Your journey is from glory to glory, from wisdom to wisdom, ever onward, upward, and Godward.

There is no death. If a light bulb goes out, do you say, "That's the end of electricity," or do you insert another bulb? Electricity is. It was here before Jesus, Moses, Elijah, Mohammed or Buddha walked the earth. So was the idea of the principle of radio, or television, or submarines, or airplanes. They could have used these things, but the idea didn't come to them. They didn't think it was possible. They were human, like all of us. They were born, like all of us. It may be that some appropriated more Divinity than others. They were all born, like all of us, for all humans are children of God. What else could they be? There is only one life, one Spirit. We are all children of the One. That's why all religions of the world say, "Our Father." We have a common Progenitor, the Life Principle.

That's why, when you radiate love, peace, and goodwill to another, you are selfish; because you are blessing yourself. When you hurt another you hurt yourself. Subjectively we are all one; objectively we seem to be somewhat different. Just like the various countries in the world. Above the ocean, they all seem to be different. Underneath there is a unitary wholeness. They are all connected deep down in the ocean. Likewise, subjectively we are all one. To hurt another is to hurt yourself; to bless another is to bless yourself. When you radiate love, peace, and goodwill to all those where you are working and to all those people in this country and every other country, you are selfish because you are blessing yourself.

There is no end to the glory that is humankind. The journey of your loved one is ever onward, upward, and Godward. You can't be less tomorrow than you are today. Life goes not backward nor tarries with yesterday. Tell me honestly: If someone is lost up in the air do you go up in the air and say, "This is where he was born," or "This is where he passed on"? No, you don't. Likewise, if many people were lost in an ocean catastrophe, do you go out in the ocean and say, "This is where they were born," or "This is where they died" with some little sign? All these things are lies. All graves are lies, because there is no one who died anyplace. There's no one buried anyplace. Do you think that Eisenhower is buried someplace, or President Kennedy? That's absurd! No one is buried anyplace. There are no graveyards except the graveyards you make in your own mind. The earthly remains may be interred, but the real person lives on.

If something happens to the piano, it is burned up, is that the end of music? Music just *is*. It transcends all instruments. You have bodies to Infinity. You'll never be without a body. You have a body now. That's why the wise and spiritually illumined person today never visits a graveyard, because there is no one there. They asked of Socrates: "Master, where will we bury you?" He looked at them and laughed, and he said, "Bury me anyplace if you can catch me." How could you bury someone anyplace? That's too stupid for words. You have bodies to Infinity, a fourth-dimensional body. You'll never be without a body; you couldn't be. You have it now. And the body undergoes dissolution; it becomes grass, hail, and snow; but there is no one buried anyplace. To go there to a grave is to identify with lack, limitation, cessation, and misery; and you create graveyards in your own mind and bring on all manner of disease. Never do it.

Give the love in your heart to your loved ones. They are right where you are. They are around you, separated by frequency only. In other words, wake up. You have another body. You have it now. It's rarefied and attenuated, enabling you to pass through solid matter. You will meet your loved ones; you will grow in wisdom, truth, and beauty. The little child whose life was snuffed out in the womb still grows and expands as a grace note in the grand symphony of all creation. It will be a beautiful girl or boy when you meet it in the next dimension, for life is growth. Life is newness, expansion. Actually, you go there every night, as I said, when you go to sleep.

If, for example, you're afraid of death, of after life, of judgment day, and things of that nature, then you are being governed by ignorance and delusion and by false beliefs of all kinds. For God has not given us the spirit of fear, but of power, and of love, and of a sound mind. Death in Biblical language is ignorance of the truth. That's the only death there is. We die only to the false beliefs, the illusions of the world, to the creeds and dogmas of the world, to the fears and the false beliefs of the world.

Every prayer is a death. You must die to what you are before you can live to what you long to be. You must die to the belief in poverty and resurrect a God of opulence in your own mind. Death in Biblical language is ignorance of the truth of God. Ignorance is the only sin, and all the misery, suffering, in this world is the result of ignorance. Buddha discovered that thousands of years ago. He asked Brahma the cause of all the suffering and misery in the world; and Brahma (which means God) answered him: Ignorance. Teach the people the truth and set them free. That's the answer he got, and that was 5,000 years B.C.

Thy rod and thy staff they comfort me. The rod. They asked Moses: What do you have in your hand? He said, the rod. And he threw it on the ground and it became a serpent, crawling. Do you crawl on the ground? Do you resurrect the Divinity within you? Do you realize one with God is a majority? Do you realize you that you can think of the Infinite now? It moves on your behalf? Or do you crawl along the ground, governed by your five senses? You catch it by its tail, you know. Moses smote the rock, and lo and behold, the water came forth. Then that rod swallowed up all the false rods of the Egyptians.

The rod is the Power of God, the Wisdom of God. When you touch that Power, call upon It. It responds to you and all the rods of the Egyptians (meaning ignorance, fear, and false beliefs) are swallowed up. So the staff represents your authority and ability to use it.

To meditate and think about the Omnipotence and Omniscience of the Infinite Presence, it brings your mind to an inner state of quietude and passivity. Think of a beautiful, quiet lake on a mountaintop and how it reflects the heavenly lights, such as the stars and the moon. Likewise, when your mind is still and quiet, you will reflect the heavenly truths and lights of God. The quiet mind gets things done. When your mind is still, quiet, and receptive, the

Divine idea or solution to your problem rises to your surface mind. That is the guidance and intuitive voice of the Infinite Presence and Power.

When the lake in the mountain is disturbed, it doesn't reflect the lights of the heavens above. When your mind is quiet, the answer comes. A quiet mind gets things done. Claim that Infinite Intelligence is guiding you now, and give thanks for the joy of the answered prayer. His rod and staff will comfort you, because there is no peace except you understand where the power is. The power is omnipotent; there is nothing to oppose It. How could you have peace except you have discovered the power? Peace comes on the heel of your discovery of the Infinite Presence and Power. There is nothing in the world to oppose It. It's omnipotent, all-powerful. Otherwise, works have no meaning. There is no power in the stars, suns, moons, voodoo, or anything of that nature. That is all based on ignorance because a scientific thinker doesn't give power to the created thing or phenomenalistic world; he gives power to the Creator.

Thou preparest a table before me in the presence of mine enemies. The enemies are your own thoughts, your fears, your self-condemnation, your jealousy, your envy, your doubts, your anger, resentment and ill will. These are real enemies; but they are in your own mind. When fear thoughts come to your mind, supplant them with faith in God and all things good. When prone to engage in some criticism, self-condemnation, the most destructive of all mental poisons, supplant these thoughts immediately with this great truth: "I exalt God in the midst of me, mighty to heal."

A young lady was making false allegations against her uncle, hoping to break a will so she could get some of the money bequeathed to him. He was angry and fighting the matter in his mind, making a nervous wreck of himself. However, when he saw what he was doing, he ceased fighting the matter in his mind and began to feed himself spiritually with the great truths of the Infinite, which, of course, is meditation. Meditation is simply to ponder upon, to consider with purpose, to get interested in, to get fascinated in, absorbed in a certain truth, so it becomes a part of you. That's all it means. There is nothing mysterious about it.

He began to think of the great truths of the Infinite. He contemplated peace, harmony, Divine right action. There is a principle of right action; there is no principle of wrong action in the world. He realized there was a Divine, harmonious solution. He stopped giving power to her. She had no power. She was full of greed and avarice and full of false beliefs. Of course, the whole thing was dissolved, and the judge dismissed it. He realized that an Infinite law of justice, truth, love and harmony reigned.

A medical doctor, a close friend of mine, said to me recently the publicity given to the wives of two prominent politicians in Washington who had developed cancer of the breast caused a great fear. Numbers of women flocked to him to test to see if they, too, had cancer. He added that he felt that fighting cancer, tuberculosis, heart disease, and so forth through propaganda on the screen, radio and print does more harm than good because what we fight in our mind we magnify. You fight nothing. He pointed out that the constant fear of cancer on the part of these women would ultimately create precisely the thing they fear.

Think instead of love harmony, health, peace, and right action. Walk in the consciousness of God's love, peace, wholeness, and perfection. You will automatically rise above these false beliefs, fears, and propaganda of the mass mind.

There is a prayer used in India by many people, which the young boy in a spiritually oriented family is taught: "I am all health. Brahma is my health." *Brahma* is a Hindu word for God. As the young boy sings this to himself many times a day, it becomes a habit. As he is impressionable and malleable he gradually builds up immunity to all sickness and disease. Instead of being taught that the night air gives him pneumonia, that God is going to punish him, he is a bad boy, and he's going to get the measles and the whooping cough, he'll never amount to anything. That's what some kids are taught today. They're like little animals.

Your children grow in the imagery and likeness of the dominant mental climate of the home. Teach them the Golden Rule and the law of love. Teach them to respect the Divinity within themselves and to respect the policemen and the teacher, and they'll respect their father and mother, too. Realize there is nothing in God's universe to fear. Cease giving power to the created thing. Stop being ignorant. Give power to the Creator. The whole universe is for you; nothing is against you.

Thou anointest my head with oil. Oil is a symbol of light, healing, praise, and thanksgiving. This means that the Infinite Healing Presence is now functioning in your behalf and the wisdom of God anoints your intellect. You are consecrated with Divine love. You have put gladness in your heart. God has anointed you with the oil of gladness.

One of the most wonderful ways to get an answer to your prayer is to imagine you are addressing the Infinite in the silence of your soul. Lull yourself to sleep with the words "Thank you, Father," over and over again, until you get the feeling of thankfulness. You don't change the Infinite by begging, beseeching, by prayer, or by anything; but when you enter into the mood of thankfulness, you are rising high in your mind to the point of acceptance, and the good things of life begin to flow to you.

You are thanking the Infinite for the answer to your prayer. As you do this, you carry a thankful attitude to the deep of yourself to the point of acceptance. You don't create harmony, peace, love, or beauty; you don't create anything. All these things are, and God never changes. God doesn't change Himself because you are a Catholic, Protestant, Jew, Muslim or Hindu, or because you belong to some religion or denomination. That is utter nonsense! You rise to the point of what's true of God. As you claim that and believe it, then your prayer is answered. But you don't change God by your prayer. That's superstition and gross ignorance.

My cup runneth over. The cup is a symbol of your heart, which, by contemplation, you can fill with the great truths of God. As you contemplate the beauty, the glory, and the wonders of the Infinite, you will automatically generate a feeling of love, peace, and joy, which fills your heart with ecstasy and rapture. You are able to pass that cup. You are able to say to others: "Drink ye all of this." Drink of love, of wisdom, power, and beauty. How can you drink of it except you have it? You can't give what you don't have.

The cup is your heart. It's not an fancy tea cup or some antique vessel in the British museum. This is metaphoric; it's a mystical cup. It belongs to all of us. You will find yourself exuding vibrancy, cordiality, geniality, and goodwill to all as you fill your soul with love. Your subconscious magnifies exceedingly what you deposit in it. Therefore, you find your good is pressed down, shaken together, and running over with the fragrance of the Infinite. You will find that God's love has completely dissolved everything negative in your subconscious, and you are as free as the wind. And goodness and mercy will follow you all the days of your life because you *dwell in the house of the Lord forever.*

As you continue to meditate and absorb these truths, you will discover that all things are working together for good. Divine love goes before you making happy and joyous your way. The harmony, peace, and joy of the Lord flow into your life and you find yourself expressing your talents at the highest possible level. You will discover that you become what you contemplate. When meditating on the truths of God, you will find that all your ways are pleasantness and all your thoughts are peace.

I will dwell in the house of the Lord forever. You are a temple of the Living God now. You are dwelling in God now. You are dwelling in heaven now, for heaven is the Infinite Intelligence in which you live, and move, and have your being. A kid of seven can understand that. God dwells within you and walks and talks in you. You dwell in the house, which is your own mind, when you regularly and systematically remind yourself many times a day that the Infinite Spirit is your guide, your counselor; that you are being constantly inspired from On High. Then you inhabit it. You look upon God as your Father, your Source of supply. You know that you will never want for any good thing in life, because He loves you and cares for you.

The tabernacle of God is with humankind. He will dwell with them; they shall be his people. And God, Himself, shall be with them and be their God. You are now rooted in the Divine. You are at home with God. He gives you rest and security. You are relaxed, at peace, completely free from fear. For where you are, God is; and you dwell with God forever. You are on a journey on the celestial ladder that knows no end. Every night of your life you go to sleep with the praise of God forever on your lips, and your journey is ever onward, upward, and Godward; from glory to glory, from octave to octave, from wisdom to wisdom, from power to power, from beauty to beauty, for there is no end to the glory which is yours now and forever more.

In a Nutshell

Meditation determines your destiny. We are always meditating. Your thoughts and feelings control your destiny. Meditation is as real and as natural as digestion, assimilation, and breathing.

God is the Living Spirit within you, the Supreme Intelligence, the Life Principle. We will not want for any good thing if we choose the Supreme Intelligence as our guide and counselor.

Meditate on whatsoever things are true, lovely, noble, and God-like. To meditate is to eat all these truths, to cogitate, to give your attention to something, to focus on something.

The shepherd in the Bible is a symbol of the guiding, healing, protective power of the Divine Presence within you. You are a good shepherd when you know and believe that God, or the Supreme Intelligence, is the only Presence and Power, Cause, and Substance within you.

Close your eyes. Become still and quiet. And gently affirm that the wisdom of God anoints your intellect and is always a lamp unto your feet; it's always a light upon your path. Look to the Infinite Presence at all times, and think, speak, act, and react from the standpoint of the Divine Center within you. Realize, know, feel, and claim that Infinite Spirit is your guide, your counselor, your boss, your senior partner; and that Divine right action governs you at all times.

If you're afraid of death, of after life, of judgment day, and things of that nature, then you are being governed by ignorance and delusion and by false beliefs of all kinds. For God has not given us the spirit of fear, but of power, and of love, and of a sound mind. Death in Biblical language is ignorance of the truth. That's the only death there is.

The tabernacle of God is with humankind. He will dwell with them; they shall be his people. And God, Himself, shall be with them and be their God. You are now rooted in the Divine. You are at home with God. He gives you rest and security. You are relaxed, at peace, completely free from fear. For where you are, God is; and you dwell with God forever.

CHAPTER SIX

The Protective 91st Psalm

The Book of Psalms is called "The Little Bible." It's a treasure-house of spiritual riches. Reading and meditating on these wonderful poems have helped people throughout history find peace, inspiration and comfort. Of the 150 Psalms in the Holy Scriptures, I have chosen the three, which I believe, are most helpful in overcoming fear and worry. In the preceding chapter, we examined the first of these, the 23rd Psalm, often called the great protective Psalm. Later in this book we'll discuss another helpful meditation, the 139th Psalm.

Now let's read and study the 91st Psalm—Psalms means songs to God, odes to the Deity. Each person has her or his identity in the Psalms. The 91st Psalm is a great source of inspiration and comfort to all men and women throughout the world. Millions meditate on it in all walks of life, and it has saved the lives of many people: those shipwrecked, lost at sea, from fires, from all manner of trouble. Thousands of people turn to this Psalm of protection for healing and in all sorts of emergencies and troubles. First, read it to get its essence, then reread it aloud. Take one verse at a time. Savor it, dwell upon it, give it your attention and devotion; think about it from all angles. Think about the meaning of each verse and know these great truths are sinking down into your subconscious mind and will be resurrected in your daily life. Just like you deposit seeds in the ground; seeds grow after their kind.

PSALM 91

He that dwelleth in the secret place of the most High
*   Shall abide under the shadow of the Almighty*
I will say of the Lord, He is my refuge and my fortress;
My God; in him will I trust Surely, He will deliver
*   thee from the snare of the fowler; and from the*
*   noisome pestilence.*
He shall cover thee with his feathers, and under his
*   wings shalt thou trust: His truth shall be thy field*
*   and buckler.*
Thou shalt not be afraid for the terror by night; nor
*   the arrow that flieth by day.*
Nor for the pestilence that walketh in darkness; nor
*   for the destruction that wasteth at noonday.*
A thousand shall fall at thy side, and ten thousand at
*   thy right hand; but it shall not come nigh thee.*

*Only with thine eyes shall thou behold and see the
    reward of the wicked.*

*Because thou hast made the Lord, which is my
    refuge, even the most High, thy habitation.*

*There shall no evil befall thee, neither shall any
    plague come nigh thy dwelling.*

*For He shall give His angels charge over thee, to keep
    thee in all thy ways.*

*Thou shall bear thee up in their hands, lest thou dash
    thy foot against a stone.*

*Thou shalt tread upon the lion and the adder; the
    young lion and the dragon shalt thou trample
    under feet.*

*Because he has set his love upon me, therefore will
    I deliver him: I will set him on high, because he
    hath known my name.*

*He shall call upon me and I will answer him: I will be
    with him in trouble; I will deliver him and honor
    him.*

*With long life I will satisfy him and show him my
    salvation.*

When you are fearful or worried, re-read the Psalm aloud. Recite it slowly and quietly, and you will dissipate, neutralize, and obliterate the fear. No one knows what you are thinking or meditating on now, as you drive along the road, as you are sitting down to breakfast. But, you see, these are thoughts and ideas, dreams, and aspirations of your own mind. You can meditate on the Only Presence and Power. God is all there is, and God is the Living Spirit within, the Only Power, Presence, Cause, and Substance. You can meditate on the fact that God is guiding you, God is with you, there is right action in your life; and that that One Power is moving through you. Then you are meditating. You are eating mentally these great truths.

This is called prayer, or meditation. To meditate is to give your attention, your devotion, to certain truths. Think about them from all angles, so that you ingest and absorb them; and they become a living part of you. That is real meditation. Then you demonstrate what you have been meditating on.

You *dwelleth in the secret place of the most High*. It means God, the Living Spirit Almighty, is within you. It's called the Most High. And the secret place, of course, is not up in the sky, but within yourself where you are dwelling upon these great truths. You contact the Infinite with your own thought. The kingdom of God is within. The kingdom of Intelligence and Wisdom and Power are all within you. You enter into the closet and you shut the door; and you pray to your Father, which is in secret; and the Father "which seeeth in secret shall reward thee openly." This simply means you shut the door of your senses; you turn your attention away from the problem, the difficulty, the lawsuit, or whatever it is; and you focus all your attention on the Infinite Intelligence, the wisdom and the power of the Infinite within you. Realize It is flowing through you, responding to your claim, for whatever you claim and feel to be true, the Spirit of the Almighty will move in your behalf and bring it to pass and the solution will come. That is the secret place where you go and claim and feel what you are praying for—feel is true, knowing It will respond. Whatever you claim and feel to be true will come to pass. You will be rewarded openly. For the inside governs the outside.

To abide under the shadow of the almighty means to live under the envelope of God's love. God is love; that love surrounds and enfolds you now. As you claim it, and as you recognize it, as you call to it, it turns to you. *Draw nigh to God, and He will draw nigh to you.* The whole armor of God surrounds you and enfolds you, and envelopes you.

You are immersed in the Holy Omnipresence, and the Overshadowing Presence watches over you at all times. Realize God's love surrounds you, which the impregnable fortress is within you as you dwell in the secret place, as you contemplate the Presence of God where you are. Then you are rendered impervious to all harm. You are invincible and invulnerable, for that's the impregnable fortress. No one can lay siege to it there, for one with God is a majority. If God be for you, who can be against you? For there is only One Power; It's the Almighty Power.

Shade in the Far East, where the Bible was written, represented protection from the sun. The shade, of course, was a sanctuary, the shadow of a great rock in a weary land. People would look for a great rock walking in the desert or going through the desert with their camel, because the rock would protect them from that broiling sun beating down upon the desert.

The Psalmist says Almighty, the One Power, the All Powerful One, the Ever Living One, the All Wise One, the All Knowing One. Nothing to oppose it, thwart it, or vitiate it. It's the Self-Renewing One; and with God all things are possible. He that dwelleth—this means that you are frequently contacting the Infinite within you. Like you dwell in your house, or your home. You spend most of your time there. You eat there, you sleep there, and you maybe work there. That's your habitation,

Frequent habitation of the mind simply means that you are constantly thinking of the Infinite Presence and Power guiding you, directing you, watching over you, sustaining you, and strengthening you, realizing It's your guide, your counselor, your adjuster, your troubleshooter, your paymaster. It's the healing agency within you. You are always looking to it for guidance and for right action. *In Him we live, and move, and have our being.* God lives, moves, and has his meaning in us.

So that's your realization of that. Then you are dwelling in that secret place of the Most High. You are dwelling there because of frequent habitation of the mind of these great truths. Think about this Presence frequently during the day. Realize you are dwelling in the Infinite now. Regularly and systematically claim: "Infinite Intelligence guides, directs, and watches over me." Make a habit of this, and you could be said to dwell in that secret place of the Most High.

Many people pray when sick or when trouble comes, but if you pray regularly, you will avoid the trouble. Meditate regularly on this Psalm. Charge your mental and spiritual batteries.

To meditate, as I said, means to give your attention to the great truths of God. Absorb them, digest them, and let them sink into your soul. *I will say of the Lord, He is my refuge and my fortress: my God; in him will I trust.* The Lord is God, as the Psalmist says, the Sovereign Power, the Living Spirit Almighty. There is only One Power, not two or three. You trust this Presence, which means you give it your allegiance, loyalty, recognition, knowing there is no other. The minute you give power to any created thing on the face of the earth, you cease to worship the One Who Forever Is. Then you have a false god. You are giving greater power to the created thing rather than the Creator, which is absurd, of course.

God is Pure Spirit. There is no other power. You trusted your mother when you were young. She had you in her arms, and you knew she wouldn't throw you into the fire. You looked into her eyes, and you saw love there. Likewise, all the love in the world is a faint reproduction of that Infinite ocean of love, for God is love.

Affirm frequently: "I am inspired from On High. God loves me, for it is written: *He careth for me.*" As you constantly claim that God is the Only Presence, Power, Cause, and Substance, guiding, directing, governing, and sustaining you, then after a while it will become your Lord, your master, your dominant conviction.

Your subconscious mind accepts the dominant of two ideas. This dominant conviction that God's love and God's peace are saturating your mind and heart will govern all your lesser thoughts, actions, and reactions; and you will lead a charmed life. You trust the Infinite regardless of appearances, for He never faileth. The mere fact that you are meditating on this Psalm indicates you have faith and that you trust the Presence and the Power. Your faith and confidence is in God's healing love instead of the ailment, or the negative condition, or the impending lawsuit.

You are told: *Surely, he shall deliver thee from the snare of the fowler, and from the noisome pestilence. He shall cover thee with his feathers, and under his wings shalt thou trust: his truth shall be thy shield and buckler. Surely, he shall deliver thee from the snare.* Here is a definite assurance that your prayer will be answered in ways you know not of, for as the heavens are above the earth, so are my ways above your ways, and my ways are not your ways.

The snare of the fowler and the noisome pestilence— this could mean deception, trickery, or someone trying to undermine you; or it could also mean fear of the flu, or the virus, or something of that nature. You are, however, to have no fear or doubt, for you have received the Divine antibody, the conviction of God's love and God's guidance surrounding you at all times.

Under his wing shalt thou trust. This is, of course, symbolic. God is the Living Spirit without face, form, or figure. *Wings* mean protection. The hen gathers her chickens under her wings to protect them; so does the mother bird.

His truth shall be thy shield and buckler. You shall know the truth, and the truth shall set you free. God is truth, God is all-powerful, and the realization of your desire today is the truth that will set you free. If you are sick, health will free you. If you are poor, wealth will free you of your problem. If you were in prison, freedom would be your savior.

One with God is a majority. The joy of the Lord is your strength. If God be for you, who can be against you? *Thou shalt not be afraid for the terror by night; nor for the arrow that flieth by day.* Night means darkness. Fear is a shadow in the mind created by ourselves, created by our own thoughts, generated by ourselves. The things we fear do not exist; they have no reality. They are shadows in our minds. Most fear comes from the fact that external things are causative, which is the big lie. An external thing is an effect; it's not a cause. One condition doesn't create another. One circumstance doesn't create another. Everything is subject to change. As you change your mind, you change your body and your environment.

You are told that your enemies are of your own household. The enemy is fear, doubt, resentment, and hostility. These are of your own mind, generated by ourselves. You are the creator of your worry; you are the creator of your fear. You can also contemplate God's love, peace, harmony, right action; then fear goes away. When fear comes, affirm: "God's love fills my soul. God's peace floods my mind." Then the fear goes away. What happens to the darkness when you turn on the light? Darkness is the absence of light. Turn on the light in your own mind. Affirm: "God loves me and cares for me."

The *arrow that flieth by day*; and the destruction that wasteth at noonday. The arrow is any negative thought, the world, the propaganda, the news, the headlines, and things of that nature. Fear thoughts. Also, it could refer to sickness, or problems in the office, inharmonious human relations. Day means light, and night means darkness, as we said. Meaning that you are aware of the problem, the difficulty; that the light shines on it. In other words, when the sun is shining you can see things better than when the night comes. It means you are aware of that problem and you can meet it head on. The problem is divinely outmatched. The problem is there, but God is there, too; and God knows only the answer. God is the Infinite Intelligence within you, not an anthropomorphic being up in the skies, a glorified sort of a man. That's absurd, childish. That's being immature. That's living in the jungle.

The *pestilence that walketh in darkness* could refer to some subconscious resentment, suppressed rage or anger, some prejudice. Prejudice means pre-judgment. I have judged before I know anything about it. Prejudice means I'm down on what I'm not up on. It may refer to some poison pocket in the subconscious mind like jealousy, called the green-eyed monster. It's one of the most destructive mental poisons there is. Envy is another destructive poison.

Most of the difficulties are due to subconscious patterns of false religious beliefs, such as guilt. Guilt is called the curse of curses. Nobody is punishing you but yourself. Forgive yourself, and you are forgiven. Life always forgives. Life never punishes; it can't. The Absolute can't punish. All judgment is given to the son. The son is your own mind. You are passing judgment on yourself. You are punishing yourself.

Feed your subconscious mind with life-giving patterns and you obliterate all the negative patterns, wipe them out, for the lower is subject to the higher. Supposing you had a pail of dirty water in your home and you began to pour clean water into it. The moment comes when you have clear, pure water. That's prayer. Filling your mind with the truths of God, you crowd out of your mind everything unlike God, so you won't be afraid for the pestilence that walketh in darkness; nor for the destruction that wasteth at noonday.

If people are plotting against you or trying to undermine you, or trying to sell you a shady deal of some kind, these would refer to the pestilence that walketh in darkness. Any negative activity inimical to your welfare (such as you are in a corporation and people are trying to undermine you or lie about you, or things of that nature), you would know about it. You would realize that the love, the light, and the glory of the Infinite surrounds you and enfolds you. The whole thing would be dissolved because faith in God and all things good would protect you.

God's love saturates your whole being, giving all your allegiance to the One Power; not to other men or women. Because if you give power to other humans, you'd say, "They are gods," new gods that you have. You would be making them greater than God. Wouldn't that be absurd? Wouldn't you be unjust to yourself? Wouldn't it be a form of insanity to give power to other people?

Thou art my hiding place; thou hast preserved me; thou shalt compass me about with songs of deliverance. How could you lose with that attitude of mind? I know a detective who, every morning of his life, says, "Thou art my hiding place; thou hast preserved me; thou shalt compass me about with songs of deliverance." He has said this so frequently—at night prior to sleep and in the morning before he goes to work—that his soul is saturated with it, and he has built up an immunity. He has been shot at, they've thrown grenades at him, sometimes point blank they have aimed a gun at him; and somehow nothing ever happened to him.

Nothing ever will, because he has built up this immunity through the 91st Psalm. Through saying to himself, "Thou art my hiding place; thou hast preserved me; thou shalt compass me about with songs of deliverance." You have that deliverance also, There is only One Power that delivers you; not two, only one.

A thousand shall fall at thy side, and ten thousand at thy right hand; but it shall not come nigh thee. As you fill your mind with the eternal truths of God, you will crowd out of your mind everything unlike the One Who Forever Is. Right means the objective world. Your spiritual thoughts destroy the negative thoughts. One spiritual thought destroys ten thousand negative thoughts, and you will also neutralize all the negative patterns in your subconscious mind. Ten thousand at thy right hand: these are the negative thoughts. If you are thinking constructively, harmoniously, and peacefully, these negative thoughts come in and out and find no pastures. They have no effect upon you.

Only with thine eyes shalt thou behold and see the reward of the wicked. The eyes mean the objective world you are looking at. Of course, you realize there is a lot of evil in the world. There is no principle of evil, but people commit evil. There are crime and sickness. We experience man's inhumanity to man. The jails and hospitals are full of people: psychotics, schizophrenics, sex maniacs. People commit murder. Surely, they do all these things. You are aware of that, but you say: "Well, I'm not going to get involved, agitated, perturbed, and excited. I might get ulcers, high blood pressure, or something else."

If you get terribly agitated, you could get a stroke, you know. That's no way to live. Where there is no opinion, there is no suffering. You are not responsible if a person is psychotic, or a hardened criminal. You are walking in the consciousness of God's love, and God's peace, and God's harmony. Then you are contributing to the peace and harmony of the whole. You are radiating the sunshine of His love, and the whole world is blessed because you walk this way. But if you go forth with anger, rage, hate, and all the rest of it, you are pouring out more mental poisons on the mass mind. Yes, more toxins. And you are contributing to the negation of the world.

Only with thine eyes. Yes, you are detached from it. You are not getting absorbed in it. You realize it is there, and you bless them all and walk on. But you are not going to get contaminated with it. Where there is no opinion, there is no suffering; where there is no judgment, there is no pain. Let your opinion lie still. Maintain a calm, peaceful mind. What good would a doctor be without a steady hand when operating, and a mind at peace? What good would an emotionally disturbed and agitated psychologist is to you? If surgeons have an infected finger, they can't operate. When doctors suffer a bad cold, they don't see patients. Maintain your peace, inner serenity, and tranquility. Keep in tune with the Infinite; then you can help the world. The mind at peace gets things done.

Only with thine eyes shalt thou behold and see the reward of the wicked. Then you know that when people misuse the law, the law punishes them. *Vengeance is mine: I will repay, saith the Lord.* Only with thine eyes shalt thou behold and see the reward of the wicked. Fret not about evildoers or the workers of iniquity. They shall be cut down. The law takes care of people if they are misusing it.

Exalt God in the midst of you. The wicked means those who are bewitched or using the law negatively. The law of the Lord is perfect. The mills of the gods grind slowly, but they grind exceedingly fine.

Because thou hast made the Lord, which is my refuge, even the most High, thy habitation; there shall no evil befall thee, neither shall any plague come nigh thy dwelling. Frequent habitation of the mind that God dwells within you, walks and talks in you, and keeping in tune with the Infinite, then no evil shall befall you. This is a definite promise of the response of Infinite life and love.

Turn to the Divine Presence as your refuge by constantly claiming: "God loves me and cares for me." Do it regularly; then it's frequent habitation of the mind, which performs a miracle. The promise in the Bible is always a law. And a law means the way a thing works. So there is a response of the Infinite Intelligence to you. Call upon me, I will answer you; I'll be with you in trouble.

I will set him on high, because he hath known my name. The *name* means the nature, and the nature of Infinite Intelligence is responsiveness. If you ask for bread, I will not give you a stone. If you ask for a fish, I will not give you a serpent. Meaning you get a response according to the nature of your request. It becomes the embodiment of your ideal. It's a law like Boyle's Law, Rome's Law, or any other law. Whatever you impress is expressed. That's the law of mind.

He shall give his angels charge over thee, to keep thee in all thy ways. Angel comes from Angelus, a messenger, a messenger of God; ideas, monitions, feelings, flashes of illumination come into one's mind.

At one of my lectures, a man told me that one day he was driving along the road and suddenly stopped. He said, "I didn't know really why, but I was compelled to, and I turned into the side of the road off the main road." He said, "Immediately, a drunkard came around the corner. He was going 80 miles an hour. He was right in my lane. A collision would have taken place, and probably both of us would have been killed."

This man, before he gets in the car in the morning to go to work, reads the 91st Psalm out loud three times. It is a great protective psalm. Then the angels, the guiding principle within him, the wisdom of his subconscious mind prompted him. It was sort of a compulsion within him, and he followed the lead. He didn't suppress it; he didn't reject it. And he didn't keep on driving. He answered, he responded.

The angel is the Angelus, the guiding principle, the idea that pops into your mind that guides you in your relationship with people. It also guides you in your diet, in your investments, in right activity, in your relationships with all people. Say, "Infinite Intelligence guides me in all my ways." That means in all directions. If you are taking the wrong kind of food, it guides you that way, too; and you stop taking the food that contributes to your adiposity. It guides you in your relationship with people, in your chosen work. It guides the hand of surgeons when they operate. Declare: "God is guiding me now." It will guide you to say the right thing at the right time. If you are wondering what to say to a person, say, "Infinite Spirit reveals to me the right words for this occasion," and the words will be given to you at that time.

These are the monitions, the warnings, the ideas that well up from the depths of yourself. These angels charge over thee, to keep thee in all thy ways. When the con man is trying to sell you something that doesn't exist or asking you to take your money out of the bank and double it, or he tells you you are going to get 20 percent interest, why doesn't he tell all his relatives? Why doesn't he invest himself? Why does he come to you? Because he thinks you are gullible and that he can brainwash you, and mesmerize you, and hypnotize you, and make a fool of you. If you are saying,

"God is guiding me in all my ways; the light shines in me," immediately you have an inner feeling, an inner silent knowing of the soul that the whole thing is phony. And you don't give him a dime. Why doesn't he take the 20 percent himself? If this gold mine is going to make a fortune for you, why doesn't he buy the gold mine himself and keep the fortune for himself? For the simple reason that he doesn't believe a word of what he is saying. Maybe he is making a hundred dollars a week, and he is going to tell you how to get a thousand a week. Well, if his method or technique will make a thousand dollars a week for you, why doesn't he do it for himself?

Claim guidance. Claim that the angels will watch over you. They don't have wings. It's intelligence, and wisdom, and a power within you that responds to you. It's a predominant hunch, an inner feeling. It's an idea that wells up in your mind.

Thou shalt tread upon the lion and the adder; the young lion and the dragon shalt thou trample under feet. The lion is that great obstacle, that great depth, that great problem which is very acute. Daniel in the lion's den? Well, the lion might be the so-called incurable disease. There are incurable people; there are no incurable diseases. There are certain people who are absolutely convinced they can't be healed, and according to their belief is it done unto them. It's that insuperable obstacle, that great obstacle that you think, or that great debt or something.

But you are told: "Daniel turned away from the lion. He turned to the light within," meaning that Supreme Intelligence within, which knows only the answer and knows the way out. It knows how to bring a solution to the most complex problem in the world. You may be in a lion's den of obstacles or difficulties. You say, "Look at all these bills; I can't pay them." Turn to the God Presence within; don't think of the bills, or the difficulties, or the obstacles, and all that. Don't think of any sum of money; don't think of any particular date. Go to the Source and say, "God is the Source of my supply, and all my needs are met at every moment of time and point of space. God's wealth is circulating in my life, and there is always a surplus."

Great peace have they that love thy law, and nothing shall offend them. It is done unto me, as I believe. And all things are ready if the mind be so. And according to my faith is it done unto me. And I will restore health unto thee, and I will heal thee of thy wounds, saith the Lord. Call upon me and I will answer you. I'll be with you in trouble. I'll set you on High because you have known my name.

The lion and the adder: The adder means a complex, a hidden fear. Oh, it could also mean dissociation like splitting, multiple personality, and things of that nature, all of which, of course, are subjective. It could mean also the schizophrenic, the paranoiac, and so forth. The lion is ferocious, of course, pitiless. But the lion faces you. It doesn't snap at you like a snake. It's not a snake, in other words as a snake, hidden in the jungle, strikes when you don't expect it.

The lion and the adder mean complexes a person has, the fears, the multiple personalities where three or four people seem to speak all at once, or at different times. All this, of course, represents complexes. Complex means a group of negative thoughts charged with fear, hidden in the recesses of the subconscious mind.

Thou shalt tread upon the lion. The young lion and the dragon shalt thou trample under feet, meaning that as you claim the Presence of God, the Divine love, Divine peace, and Divine harmony saturate your mind and your heart. The lower is subject to the higher. Then you are cleansing the stable that has been dirty perhaps for forty years. For the lower is subject to the higher. Love casts out hate, peace casts out pain, and joy casts out sadness. Divine love, Divine peace, and the miraculous Healing Power go straight to the roots of the trouble; then you are redeemed.

Today, of course, much emphasis is placed on subconscious fixation, compulsions, and all that. These represent the lion and the adder, the dragon. Shalt trample, meaning contemplating the Presence of God dissolves all that. The real trouble is in your conscious mind, really, for there is no error in the subconscious that is not under the control of the conscious mind. Surely, these problems are in the subconscious, but they can be controlled, and they can be eliminated. The subconscious is subject to the conscious mind. Your feelings are subject to your thoughts. Even false beliefs, religious beliefs, supposing they were foisted upon you when you were a child, you can still obliterate them by changing your opinions and beliefs now. You can begin to believe in a God of love, One Presence, One Power (not two), no Devil, no hooves and horns.

Your old fear abides because you still hold a philosophy that sustains it. If you believe in a power other than the Infinite, then you are in trouble. This is the root of all fear, the root of all multiple personalities, the basis of all schizophrenics, and everything else. When you disabuse your mind of this error, you have cut the pipeline that nourishes the neurotic tendencies in your subconscious mind. Prayer is a great changer of all things, because it changes your consciousness, which makes all things. Don't beg an anthropomorphic being in the sky to pass a miracle for you. Recast your thoughts. There is only One Power, which is Spiritual. It is your own consciousness. Realize It is sovereign and supreme.

As the love, the light, and the glory of the Infinite flow through you in transcendent loveliness, then you will dethrone, exorcise, and banish all the tormentors in your mind. Then you are treading on the lion and the adder; the dragon you are trampling under feet. Magnificent truth.

Because he hath set his love upon me, therefore will I deliver him: I will set him on high, because he hath known my name. Love is not an emotion, not a sentiment. When you tune in on the Infinite in recognition, realizing it is all-powerful. It is all love, and light, and truth, and beauty. When you give your loyalty to this Presence and power; when you insist on harmony, which is your real desire, you will not accept anything less. You will not compromise, you insist on harmony, you insist on health, you insist on peace; you give all your allegiance, all your loyalty to the One Power, then you are said to love God.

If you love me, He said, keep my commandments. The mere fact that you pray and that you turn to the Infinite, or that you are listening to this Psalm (that is, the inner meaning of it), it indicates love, recognition. Love in the Bible is your recognition, your acceptance of One Power. It means your mind is pure, because you are giving allegiance to the One Power, not two or three.

I will set him on high, because he hath known my name. The *name* is the nature of something. The nature of the Infinite is omnipotence. It's omniaction, It's all powerful, boundless love, infinite intelligence, absolute harmony. It's all-wise. Then you are recognizing its name, or its nature. If it's all-powerful, there is nothing to challenge it. This is to set on high, that is, above difficulties, problems. This assures you your freedom, because you know the nature of it is to respond.

To know is not an intellectual apprehension; it's a degree of understanding like you know the laws of chemistry, or the laws of physics. It's your realization, so you know that you mix certain things together, put sodium in water, you'll get sodium hydroxide. You know it. You have no particular feeling about it. You are teaching mathematics, and you say: "Nine times nine is 81." Well, you have no particular feeling about it. You have knowledge, you know. And if the child puts down: "3 + 3 = 7" on the blackboard, you teach that 3 and 3 are 6. You have a certain satisfaction, a certain understanding.

Likewise, to know the God Presence is to know it is supreme, omnipotent. There is no doubt in your mind about it. It's the only Power there is.

He shall call upon me, and I will answer him: I will be with him in trouble; I will deliver him, and set him on high, because he hath known my name. I will honor. With long life will I satisfy him, and show him my salvation. When you call, that simply means that before you call the answer is known. It was known in Divine mind, which knows all things. It's the All-Wise One, the All Knowing One, the Self-Renewing One. The modern scientist and astrophysicist know that before you call, the answer is there. It doesn't make any difference whether it's a mathematical problem, geological problem, or a problem of astrophysics. The answer is known to the Infinite Intelligence. Therefore, you contemplate the answer, knowing that you have the answer; and the answer then will flow through you.

I will deliver him, and honor him, meaning that deliverance will come—the solution to your problem will come—because you recognize it as supreme and omnipotent. You recognize its nature as responsiveness.

With long life will I satisfy him, and show him my salvation. A long life means a life of peace, of harmony, of joy, wisdom, and understanding. You may live to be 90 or 100 years of age, but if half the time is in a hospital with pains and aches, that's not a long life in Bible language. A long life in the Bible is the life of peace, harmony, creativity, and joy. It's the life abundant.

Salvation is a solution to your problem, no matter what it is. It's an old Hindu word meaning salvation, solution to any problem in the world. Your prayer conforms to the Divine will when it is constructive, when it blesses you, and conforms to Universal Principle.

A wonderful prayer would be:

I dwell in the secret place of the Most High, and I abide in the shadow of the Almighty. As I contemplate God in His glory and His wonders within me, I abide in the shadow always, because I know God's love surrounds me and enfolds me, making straight, beautiful, and joyous my way. The Lord, the Spiritual Power, is sovereign and supreme, the Only Power. It responds to my thought. It is, therefore, my refuge and my fortress. This Spiritual Power inspires, heals, strengthens, and restores my mind and body. It is God. It is beneficent. It's a kindly Power. I trust it completely. It responds as mercy, love, inspiration, and beauty. This Divine Power covers me with its feathers of love, light, and peace. It is wonderful. I completely reject the negative thoughts of the world, the arrow by day. God's love dissolves the fear patterns of my subconscious, the terror by night. I know I am secure in the invisible hands of God. I always vibrate with the mind of God, and all is well. I am completely free from fear of accidents or hostile activities, the pestilences that walketh in darkness; because I know I am immunized and God-intoxicated. I have received the Divine antibody, the Presence of God, in my heart. The thousands of negative thoughts and suggestions of the world are destroyed consciously and subconsciously, for God walks and talks in me, and I live in the joyous expectancy of the best. There shall no evil befall thee, neither shall any plague come nigh thy dwelling. God and His holy angels, meaning God's ideas, impulses, intuition, and guidance have complete charge over me, and I am safeguarded in all my ways: in health, right activity, self-expression, and Divine companionship.

By contemplating the Presence of God, you tread upon the lion and the adder, and the Presence of God is the presence of peace, harmony, joy, love, abundance, light, and truth. Then you tread upon the lion and the adder, the obstacles and complexes of all kinds. Your salvation, or solution, is revealed to you as you think of the Infinite, the only Presence and Power, Cause, and Substance. Then all the Divine forces hasten to minister to your eternal joy. That Lordly Presence is your shepherd, and you sing the song of the jubilant soul for you have chosen God as your guide, counselor, and way-shower. And you are always in the shadow of the Almighty. Divine Intelligence rules and guides you in all your ways. You shall never want for peace, harmony, or guidance; because God's wisdom governs you. You lie down in green pastures always, since God is prospering you beyond your fondest dreams. You find yourself beside the still waters as you claim the infinite peace of God floods your mind and your heart. Your emotions (waters) are still and calm. Your mind is serene. It reflects God's heavenly truths and light. Your soul is restored. Think of God's Holy Presence within you all day long, the Infinite Which lies stretched in smiling repose. That's the Infinite Presence and Power, the Living Spirit Almighty. You walk the paths of righteous through your devotion and attention to God's eternal verities. You know there is no death, for you fear no evil. God has not given you the spirit of fear, but of love, power, and a sound mind.

The banquet table of God is always set before you. It is the secret place of the Most High, where you eat of the great nourishing truths of God, where you walk and talk with the Infinite; and you eat these nourishing truths this way, as you contemplate the bread of peace, love, faith, and joy. So you say: "My faith is in God and all things good. I believe in the goodness of God in the land of the living. I believe in the guidance of God, and God is guiding me now." Then you are spreading the banquet table in your own mind; you are eating the truths of God. You say, "I am inspired from On High; the Spirit of the Almighty moves on the waters of my mind." And the meat that you eat is the Omnipotence of God; the wine that you drink is the essence of joy; and the bread that you eat is the bread of peace, harmony, and joy. *Lord, ever more give us this bread.*

The wisdom of God anoints your intellect. It is a lamp unto your feet; it's a light upon your path. Your cup (your heart) is truly a chamber of God's Presence. It runneth over with love and joy. You mentally dwell on goodness, truth, and beauty. You are dwelling in the house of God at all times.

Forgiveness must take place within your heart and mind to be the real thing. To *forgive* means to "give for." Give yourself the feeling of love and goodwill, instead of the mood of anger, resentment, or hatred. Your mental attitude governs your experience. Keep your mind clear, poised, serene, and calm, and full of the expectancy of the best. If you resent another, you are giving too much power to that other and you are hurting yourself. Remember, *I will say of the Lord, he is my refuge and my fortress; my God, in Him will I trust.* You turn to the God Presence. That is your Source as the guide, as the Source of all your blessings. Don't look to somebody else. God is the Source of guidance, prosperity, peace, and harmony. Why would you look to another? Why would you say, "He's blocking my good"? Why would you have resentment? You see, this law does away with all cause of resentment, because you can go to the Living Spirit within you and claim your good. Believe in the reality of this Presence and Power; it will respond to you. Then you can, too, have the unqualified capacity to go within yourself and claim health, happiness, peace, abundance, and security.

Why should you be jealous of anyone? Why envious? You can go to the eternal Source. Where did the other person get it? You go to the Source of all and claim it. It's impersonal, no respecter of persons. It will respond to you, too.

As the Psalmist said, Call upon me, I will answer you: I will be with you in trouble. I will deliver you; deliver you from poverty, too, from pain, from sickness, from confusion, from jail, or from being lost in the woods. It will lead you out. To forgive, therefore, is to change your thoughts. Forgive yourself, and keep it changed.

Use the following technique wholeheartedly, sincerely, and lovingly. "I pray as follows for the other person. I surrender the other person to God." This is one way, too, of getting rid of the lion and the adder, you know—that complex that's within you. If there is some suppressed rage, or resentment, or poison pocket in your subconscious, this is a wonderful way to get rid of it. For example, if you have resentment against a former spouse, say, "I surrender that person to God completely. The peace of God fills his (her) soul. He (she) is inspired and blessed in all his (her) ways. Any time I think of him (her), I will say, 'I released you; God be with you.'" And after a while you will meet that person in your mind, and you'll be at peace.

If you are sizzling over something someone did now, or if someone comes into your mind and you sizzle, then, you see, the adder is there, snaps at you. It could come forth as a growth or some problem in your mind, you see. The way to tread upon it is to fill your mind with love. Say, "God's love fills my soul. I surrender that person to God completely. I wish for that person health, happiness, peace, and all the blessings of life." For the other is yourself, and what you withhold from another, you withhold from yourself. Then wonders will begin to happen in your life, because the person, you see, is not out there. The person is a thought-image in your mind. It is browbeating, intimidating you, and robbing you of vitality, enthusiasm, and energy, making you a physical and mental wreck. And who is it hurting? It's hurting you. The other person is on the Mediterranean, or dancing under the midnight stars on a beautiful ship. Look what you are doing to yourself.

Resentment is the quickest way in the world to get old, and the quickest way in the world to establish mental and spiritual trouble in your mind and in your body. It is the quickest way in the world, too, to be depleted and to become a mental and a physical wreck. Stop robbing yourself of vitality, enthusiasm, and energy. Realize God's love fills your soul; God's peace floods your mind. You will say of the Lord, "He is your refuge, your fortress; my God, in Him will I trust. He will deliver me from the snare of the fowler and from all negativity, for I walk and talk with Him." Then wonders will begin to happen in your life.

Realize the Lord is your pilot. You shall not drift. These are the angels that watch over you to keep you in all your ways. Mariners use it, naval officers use it, and pilots in the plane use it. They realize that there is a Guiding Principle that will guide them through the storm, through the turbulence, through the lightning, and through the storm at sea, too. Say to yourself, too:

The Lord is my pilot. I shall not drift. He lighteth me across the dark waters. He steereth me in the deep channels. He keepeth my log. He guideth me by the star of holiness for His name's sake. Yea, though I sail with the thunders and tempests of life, I shall dread no danger, for thou art with me. Thy love and thy care, they shelter me. Thou preparest a harbor before me in the homeland of Eternity. Thou anointest the waves with oil. My ship rideth calmly. Surely, some light and starlight shall favor me on the voyage I take, and I will rest in the port of my God forever.

Angels have charge over thee. *They shall bear thee up lest thy dash thy foot against a stone*, meaning lest you hurt yourself in any way, shape, or form, you'll be protected. Therefore, it will prevent you from stumbling, making the wrong decision; because you realize the Guiding Principle is watching over you. The *Lord doth go before thee* when you drive. The angel will watch over you, too; because your dominant mood of faith and confidence is that God's wisdom and God's power rule, guide, and govern you in all your ways. This feeling, this awareness, is the Lord, or the dominant conviction that goes before you. Your conviction of God's Presence is strong and mighty, and you know the spiritual atmosphere in which you dwell goes before you making straight, beautiful, joyous, and happy your way. Know that whenever you travel by bus, train, airplane, automobile, or whatever means of conveyance you use. God's love and intelligence guide and govern your journey.

All the highways and byways of your world are controlled by God, making the skies above and the earth beneath a highway for your God. That's one of the meanings of He shall give his angels charge over thee, to keep thee in all thy ways. These angels are ideas, impulses, monitions, flashes of illumination that come into your mind; and they will bear you up, protect you, lest you dash your foot against a stone, lest you make any error or any mistake. Claim it, believe it, and make a habit of it.

Saturate your mind with this psalm, interspersed, of course, with the 23rd. Realize that God's circle of love is always around you and watching over you, sustaining, and strengthening you, The Lord is your light and your salvation; whom shall you fear? The Lord is the strength of your life; of whom shall you be afraid? This is the Lord spoken of in the 91st Psalm, the Lordly Power, the God Presence, Which is always your refuge. Turn to it. *Draw nigh unto me and I'll draw nigh unto you.* I love them that love me. Those that seek me early shall find me. Regarding the works of my hand, command ye me. A merry heart doeth good like a medicine, but a broken spirit drieth the bones.

You are ever joyous, ever active, ever energetic. You are always passing on God's ideas, because you are always calling upon this Presence. It's always answering you. It's giving you the right words for the occasion. It's inspiring you, guiding you, revealing to you truths you never knew before. It's delivering you from all sorts of problems. It's honoring you, exalting you; because you are here to grow, to expand. And you are ever joyous, ever active, and ever energetic. You are always passing on God's ideas to other people; and you are giving them peace, joy, and happiness. *In thy presence is fullness of joy; in Him there is no darkness at all. My peace I leave you; my peace I give you. Not as the world giveth, give I unto you. Heretofore you have asked for nothing; now ask that your joy might be full. These things*

*have I said unto thee, that my joy might remain in you and
your joy might be full.*

The joy of the Lord is your strength. The joy of the
Lord is your strength, too. You are always cheerful, free,
full of happiness. You have dominion over all things in
your world. You sense and feel your oneness with God, life,
the universe, and all things. You meditate on whatsoever
things are true, lovely, wonderful, and God-like. Realize
you are a child of God, and the children of God shouted
for joy. Above all things, realize now that you are dwelling
in the secret place of the Most High, and you abide in the
shadow of the Almighty. You are always watched over by
the overshadowing Presence, because you are thinking of
God. And to think of God is the greatest prayer in all the
world, for God is the Infinite, the only Presence, the only
Power, the only Cause, the only Substance, the Ever Living One, the All Wise One, the All Knowing One, the Self-
Renewing One. The contact is with your thought, and when
your thoughts are God's thoughts, God's power is with
your thoughts of good. Then no evil shall befall you; no
plague shall come nigh thy dwelling. A wonderful truth—a
promise in the Bible, you see, is the law. And the law never
changes. It remains the same yesterday, today, and forever.
Then you say of the Lord, He is your refuge, your fortress.
You say, My God, in Him will I trust. Your expectation is
from Him, Who giveth to all life, breath, and all things.

Where is your confidence today? Is your confidence in the law of the Lord? And on that law doth I meditate both day and night. Your confidence is in God, in the goodness of God in the land of the living, in the guidance of God, the abundance of God, the love of God, and the peace of God, in the justice of the Infinite. That's where your faith is; that's where your confidence is; that's where your trust is. He never fails. And *He shall cover you with His feathers and under His wing you shall rest.* And the truth of God shall be the shield and buckler. Wherever you go, you lead a charmed life, for the spell of God is always around you. And God's love surrounds you, enfolds, and enwraps you. God walks and talks in you.

No matter what the problem is, no matter what the difficulty is, you will call upon it and it answers you. It will be with you in trouble, it will deliver you and honor you. With long life will it satisfy you and show you the solution to all problems, show you its salvation.

Think of this God Presence. Dwell in that secret place. Contemplate the Ever Living One, the All Wise One, the All Knowing One, the Self-Renewing One, ever the same in my inmost being, eternal, absolutely one, whole, complete, perfect, indivisible, timeless, changeless, and ageless; without face, form, or figure; that silent, brooding Presence fixed in the hearts of all people.

In a Nutshell

When you are fearful or worried, re-read the Psalm aloud, Speak it slowly and quietly, and you will dissipate, neutralize, and obliterate the fear.

Realize God's love surrounds you, which the impregnable fortress is within you as you dwell in the secret place, as you contemplate the Presence of God where you are. Then you are rendered impervious to all harm.

Affirm frequently: "I am inspired from On High. God loves me, for it is written: He careth for me." As you constantly claim that God is the Only Presence, Power, Cause, and Substance, guiding, directing, governing, and sustaining you, then after a while it will become your Lord, your master, your dominant conviction.

As you fill your mind with the eternal truths of God, you will crowd out of your mind everything unlike the One Who Forever Is. Right means the objective world. Your spiritual thoughts destroy the negative thoughts. One spiritual thought destroys ten thousand negative thoughts, and you will also neutralize all the negative patterns in your subconscious mind.

Love casts out hate, peace casts out pain, and joy casts out sadness. So, Divine love, Divine peace, and the miraculous Healing Power go straight to the roots of the trouble; then you are redeemed.

The wisdom of God anoints your intellect. It is a lamp unto your feet; it's a light upon your path. Your cup (your heart) is truly a chamber of God's Presence. It runneth over with love and joy. You mentally dwell on goodness, truth, and beauty. You are dwelling in the house of God at all times.

CHAPTER SEVEN

Why Did This Happen To Me?

W hen life does not go as planned, when misfortune strikes, when one is unhappy with the cards one is dealt, we often hear the plaint, "Why did this happen to me?" There is no easy answer to this universal question.

To accept the trials and tribulations all humankind faces, it is necessary to think God's thoughts, to think in a new way, to think of eternal verities, to think of eternal principles of life in the same manner that mathematicians would think from the principle of mathematics, navigators would think from the principle of navigation, chemists would think from the principle of chemistry, electricians would think from the principle of electricity. They know it moves from a higher to a lower potential. They learn the laws of conductivity and insulation for wiring your house.

Likewise, your mind is a principle. Therefore, you think from the God center within. You think on whatsoever things are true, whatsoever things are just, whatsoever things are lovely, whatsoever things are pure, whatsoever things are honest and of good report; think on these things. You are thinking only when you are thinking from the standpoint of the God center within. There is a principle of harmony, not of discord; there is a principle of beauty, not ugliness; there is a principle of joy, none of sadness; there is a principle of love, not of hate; there is a principle of wholeness, perfection; there is no principle of sickness. If there were no one in the entire world could ever be healed.

Realize, therefore, that when your thoughts are completely free from fear and worry. You are thinking from the standpoint of the Divine center within you; and God speaks, thinks and acts through you. Therefore, you speak in words of wisdom, truth and beauty; words of harmony, health and peace. You think, therefore, from the God center within.

Many people do not think. Millions do not think; they think that they think, but they are mistaken. Because true thinking (we are talking about constructive thinking) is completely free from fear. All fear is based upon externals are causative. Externals are an effect, not a cause. Therefore, you must remember that if we do not think for ourselves, someone else will do our thinking for us. If you do not choose your own mood, who's going to choose it for you? Newspapers? headlines? the mass mind? We are all subjective. We're all in the mass mind. We're all in tele-pathic communication with each other. The people in this world are all extensions of ourselves.

Therefore, if you do not think constructively, harmo-niously and peacefully, the world mind, or the mass mind, or the race mind will do your thinking for you. And that mass mind believes in tragedy, misfortune, sickness, dis-ease, accidents; and they indulge in hate, murder, and all sorts of things. Is that the kind of a mind you want thinking through you and in you?

That's what happens to you if you don't do your own thinking. Then these negative vibrations, or thoughts of the mass mind, move in upon you, reach a point of saturation, precipitate as accident, misfortune, sickness, disease. We have explosions in mines today; we have airplane crashes and tragedies occurring daily. It isn't that people are evil or they are bad because their submarine goes down in the ocean, or because there is a flood in some city, or because children are hurt in accidents; and explosions take place in various factories, and things of that nature. Many people lose their lives.

We say it's necessary to keep prayed up. You keep prayed up when you fill your mind, for example, of the truths of God, which crowd out of your mind everything unlike God. *Remember ye not the former things, neither consider the things of old; but this one thing I do. Forget-*

ting the things that are behind, reaching forth unto those
things that are before. I press toward the mark for the prize.

The Bible says: "Whatsoever a man soweth, so shall he reap." This means that if we plant thoughts of peace, harmony, health, beauty, prosperity, we shall reap accordingly, and that if we sow thoughts of sickness, lack, strife, and contention, we shall reap these things. We must remember that our subconscious mind is like the soil. It will grow whatever type of seed we plant in the garden of our mind. We sow thoughts, Biblically speaking, when we believe them wholeheartedly. For whatever your conscious mind really believes, your subconscious will bring to pass, whether true or false.

Unless you do your own thinking you'll be controlled by the mass mind and the mass mind believes in misfortune, sickness, calamities, and tragedies of all kinds. Therefore, you must do your own thinking.

True thinking is completely free from fear, worry, and anxiety; because you are thinking from the God center within. When your thoughts are God's thoughts, God's power is with your thoughts of good. Therefore, you don't say to another: What boiling thoughts were you thinking? Maybe they didn't have any boiling thoughts at all. Maybe they didn't do any praying of their own. And they said: I'll take what comes. Therefore, the world mind believes in sickness and disease of all kinds. And, if you do not cleanse your own mind, the world mind will not cleanse it for you.

What happens to a home when you go away for three or four months? Rats, mice and pestiferous insects come in. The paint falls off the walls, and everything goes wrong in the house because there is no habitation, no living there. You have to shampoo your mind like you shampoo your body or cleanse your body. You have to shampoo it regularly, clearly and distinctly.

Whatever we really believe with our conscious mind, our subconscious brings to pass.

A chaplain in a hospital in Massachusetts told me that a common experience she had were patients who lamented "Why did this happen to me? What did I do to deserve this? Why is God angry with me? Why is God punishing me?" I go to church regularly, I am a charitable person, I am kind-hearted. I must have done something wrong that I don't know about. That's why I am so ill.

The law of life is the law of belief. What do you believe? To believe is to accept something as true, to live in the state of being it, to be alive to something. We should believe in the goodness of God. We should live in the joyous expectancy of the best. We should believe in the guidance of God, the harmony of God, the healing power of God to make us whole, pure, relaxed and perfect.

The chaplain reported that in many cases, she prayed with patients and helped them change their beliefs "I helped them realize that the body was spiritual; that when they changed their minds, they changed their bodies.

They began to cease giving power to the sickness in their thoughts. She taught them to pray as follows: "The Infinite Healing Presence is flowing through me as harmony, health, peace, wholeness and perfection. God's healing love indwells every cell of my being. I am made whole, pure, relaxed and perfect."

She taught them to repeat this prayer frequently, knowing what they were doing and why they were doing it. Thus the conscious mind was writing these truths down in their subconscious. Whatever you impress or inscribe in your subconscious will come to pass as form, function, experience, and events. As a result of this many patients made miraculous recoveries.

The law of life is the law of belief. If you fear sickness, you attract it. The law of the Lord is perfect. You can't think one thing and produce another. The law of life is the law of belief. Trouble of any kind is nature's alarm system that we are thinking wrongly in that direction. Nothing but a change of thought can set us free.

There is a law of cause and effect operating at all times. Nothing happens to man without his mental consent and participation. You do not have to think of an accident to have it befall you. Haven't you seen a man driving a car, careening in and out, drunk? You said, "There goes an accident." Why? There's a mind behind it, there's a mood, there's an emotion behind the wheel; there's always a mind behind it. Is that mind disturbed? Is that mind emotionally disturbed? If you are emotionally disturbed, it affects your vision. You don't see so well.

OSHA, the U.S. federal government agency responsible for occupational safety investigates the causes of industrial injuries. They are particularly concerned about companies where frequent injuries occur. In addition to their engineering staff, which examines the facilities for physical defects that may cause the accidents, safety experts with training in psychology interview the workers—not just the injured persons—but all workers in the plant. They often learn that accidents are caused when employees are emotionally upset. In companies where workers have dogmatic and domineering bosses, resentment of the boss leads to negative thoughts in the worker's mind, which results in carelessness and accidents.

Misfortune, accidents and tragedies of various kinds are signs of mental and emotional disorders that have broken out into manifestation. We must train our minds to think in a new way, to turn back to God and align our thoughts and mental imagery with the Infinite life, love, truth and beauty of God. Then we become channels for the Divine.

Still your mind several times a day and affirm slowly, quietly and lovingly: "God flows through me as harmony, health, peace, joy, wholeness and perfection. God walks and talks in me. God's spell is always around me. Wherever I go God's wisdom governs me in all my ways. Divine right action prevails. All my ways are ways of pleasantness and all my paths are peace. God's love surrounds me, enfolds me and enwraps me. God walks and talks in me. I'm surrounded by the sacred circle of God's eternal love, and the whole armor of God surrounds me."

As you dwell on these eternal verities you will establish patterns of Divine order in your subconscious mind, and whatever you impress in the subconscious mind is expressed on the screen of space. Therefore, you will find yourself watched over at all times by an Overshadowing Presence—your Heavenly Father—Who responds to you when you call upon Him. The Bible says: "Call upon me, I will answer you; I'll be with you in trouble. I'll set you on high because you hath known my name."

Now, all of us should learn how the subjective self in us works. One of the great corollaries of the great law of suggestion is this: Whatever you suggest to another, you are also suggesting to yourself. When you are giving a suggestion to another, you are giving it to yourself; because you are the only thinker in your universe. And you respond to the way you think. Whatever you are wishing for the other person, you are wishing for yourself. You are always under the law of your own thought. This is the basis of the Golden Rule, which also tells you to treat your enemies well, to pray for them that despitefully use you. In other words, never dwell on ill will for anyone or against any person on the face of the earth. You do so at your own peril, because whatever you are thinking about the other you are creating in your own mind, your body, your circumstances, your pocketbook, also. That's a simple truth.

Radiate love, peace, and goodwill to everybody. Don't judge. With what judgment ye judge, ye shall be judged. Your judgment of the other is your judgment of yourself. That's the conclusion, that's your verdict in your own mind. Many people suffer from sickness, disease, accidents and misfortune because they do not think constructively. They are letting the mass mind, or the race mind, or the law of averages govern them. They're not bad people, but they refuse to think for themselves. They do not keep prayed up. They do not neutralize the mass mind.

You know very well if you read the newspapers in the morning and listen to the radio or TV at night, what do you hear about? Murder, rape, hate, jealousy, and all sorts of misfortune seem to happen to people. They tell you about all the bad things that have happened. They don't tell you about any of the good things.

Well, likewise, if you do not keep prayed up, if you do not think for yourself, the mass mind does your thinking for you. Therefore, you must ask yourself: "Am I thinking constructively, harmoniously, peacefully?" Of course, you answer that question yourself. You are what you think all day long. For as we think in out heart (subconscious mind), so we are, so do we become, and so do we express. That's the whole law. Whatever you sow in your mind, so shall you reap.

All of us are in the mass mind, the race mind, the great psychic sea. The mass mind believes in sickness, accidents, death, misfortune, and tragedies of all kinds. If we do not do our own thinking, the mass mind, the race mind, will do our thinking for us. Gradually the thoughts of the mass mind impinging on our consciousness may reach a point of saturation and precipitate as accident, sudden illness, calamity, heart attack, so-called tragedies that happen in the air, the sea. The majority of people do not think; they think they think.

You are thinking when you differentiate between that which is false and that which is real. To think is to choose. How many people are thinking? You have the capacity to say yes and no. Let your conversation be yea, yea and no, no. You say yes to the Truth of Being and you reject everything unlike God or the Truth.

If the mental instrument could not choose, you would not be an individual. You have the ability to accept and reject; you can think on whatsoever things are true, lovely, noble and Godlike all day long. There is nothing in the entire world to stop you from thinking constructively, harmoniously and peacefully. You are thinking when you know that there is an Infinite Intelligence Which responds to your thoughts and that no matter what the problem is, as you think about a Divine solution and the happy ending, you will find the subjective wisdom within you responding to you and revealing to you the perfect plan and show you the way to go. Everywhere you move today, suggestions of people in your office, in your home, radio, television and all that, or the neighbors, their thoughts and their moods are playing upon the subtle receptivity of your mind. Whether you know it or not, these impressions are going down into your mind and muddling it, and befouling it.

If a building were left unattended for any length of time, you know what would happen to it. Likewise, every morning and every night, sit down, read your Psalms. The 91st Psalm, the 27th, 23rd, 46th, and the 1st Psalm are particularly helpful. These are marvelous truths. Psalms are songs of God. You are here to cleanse your mind, to govern it, to watch over it, just the same as you cleanse your body. You give a piece of soap to a person who is dirty, and that person takes a bath. That's a suggestion of cleanliness to him or her. Well, cleanliness is next to Godliness. Therefore, we should give attention to things that are lovely and noble; we should give attention to eternal verities, the principles of life; we should discipline our thoughts. Inattention, negligence, apathy, listlessness pay dividends; but they are negative dividends, aren't they? You have to give attention to what is true, what is noble, and what is of God.

Over the years I have had many people with medical problems come to me for advice. Some have truly serious problems; others are trivial. In any case I strongly recommend their seeking professional medical help. I am not a doctor nor am I a "healer" in the sense that the prophet

Elisha, Jesus and others have been. But often I find that the true problem is not medical, but spiritual.

One of the strangest cases brought to my attention was that of a woman, who had suffered a series of illnesses over a period of time. She told me "God has it in for me; I'm a sinner. This is why I'm being punished." She also told me that she went to a man who hypnotized her, read her past. He attributed her illnesses to a life she had previously lived in which she had been an evil person who had harmed many people. As she had not been punished in that life, she was now suffering for the sins she had committed then.

Of course, that was nonsense. It only made things worse.

I explained to her an age-old truth: There is but One power, called God, the Living Spirit Almighty. Not two, or three, or a thousand. It is the Creative Intelligence in all of us that created us. This power becomes to us what we believe it to be. To the forward, I am forward; to the pure, I am pure. If you think and believe there is a God of love, then the God of love will respond to you and become a loving being to you. If you think that God is punishing you, that you must suffer, according to your thought and belief it is done unto you. But in reality you are punishing yourself. As the Bible says "It is done unto him as he believes. For as a man thinketh in his heart or subconscious mind, so is he, so does he become, so does he express."

This woman was seeking justification and alibis for her suffering. She was looking outside herself instead of realizing the source of her illness was always in her deeper mind; because nothing happens to the body except there is a pattern in the subconscious mind

I asked her to look inside herself and determine if there was something in her past about which she felt a deep sense of guilt. She confessed that she had a love affair with a married man a few years ago and that she felt guilty and should be punished. With guilt comes fear and apprehension. And with fear comes punishment. She felt that she should be punished, and she was punishing herself.

Guilt is the curse of curses. It's one of the most destructive of all emotions. And, being a destructive, negative emotion, it cannot have a constructive outlet. These emotions get snarled up in the subconscious mind and come forth as illness and disease. This unresolved remorse was the psychic wound behind her illnesses. I helped her realize that God was not punishing her, but she was punishing herself by her own thoughts. My explanation was the cure: She forgave herself, and she sat down for twenty minutes several times a day and said: "God's healing love saturates my soul, and I forgive myself for harboring these negative, destructive thoughts." Her illnesses abated and she was soon back to a full, healthy, productive life.

There is no worse suffering than a guilty conscience, and, certainly, none more destructive. This woman had been punishing herself for several years by her destructive thinking. When she ceased to condemn herself and began to claim that the Infinite healing presence was saturating her whole being, that God dwells in every cell of her body, her illnesses disappeared.

When you stand praying, forgive. Forgive yourself first. You can't give what you don't have. As she decided to forgive herself, God's healing love healed her.

In ancient times, they attributed thoughts and feelings to the heart. Today we know it is your subconscious mind. Whatever idea is emotionalized and felt as true comes to pass once it reaches the subconscious mind. Your subconscious assumptions, beliefs, convictions dictate and control all your conscious actions. Your subconscious beliefs impel, propel and compel. Whatever you sow, you reap. Your thoughts and feelings create your destiny.

You are what you think all day long. If you fail to think constructively, wisely, and judiciously, then someone else, or the mass mind will do your thinking for you and perhaps make a complete mess of your life. If you believe that God is Infinite goodness, boundless love, absolute harmony, boundless wisdom, the God Presence will respond accordingly to you by the law of reciprocal relationship; and you will find yourself blessed in countless ways. The forces of life depend on how you use them. Atomic energy is not evil; it is good or bad, depending on the way you use it. You can use atomic energy in medicine; you can drive a ship across the ocean with it. You can use electricity to kill another or to vacuum the floor. You can use water to quench a child's thirst or drown it. You can use nitric acid to paint a beautiful Madonna on the windowpane, or you can blind a person with it. The wind which blows the ship on the rocks can also carry it so safety.

The uses to which all things or objects in the world are put are determined by the thoughts and motivations of humankind. Good and evil are in our minds. Good and evil are the movements of my own, mind relative to the One Being, Forever Whole, Pure, and Immaculate in Itself. It is the human mind that determines the use of the forces and objects in the world.

The creative force is in our minds. There is no power in the manifest universe except we give power to externals. Externals are an effect; they are not a cause. The scientific thinker does not make the phenomenalistic world a cause. It's an effect. The cause is your thought and feeling.

No matter how long you might have used your mind in a negative and destructive manner, the minute you begin to use it the right way, the right results follow. Remember not the former things, nor consider the things of old. *This one thing I do: forgetting the things that are behind and reaching forth to the things that are before, I press towards the mark for the prize.*

The prize, of course, is health, happiness, peace of mind, joy, and all the good things of life. Think good, good follows; think evil, evil follows. The minute you enthrone in your mind Godlike ideas and eternal verities, they generate their own fragrance. Then your heart becomes a chalice for God's love. And the brain and the heart unite in accord and concord based on eternal verities. Then all your ways will be pleasantness and all your paths will be paths of peace.

Nothing happens by chance. Everything is pushed from behind. It's a universe of law and order; therefore, everything happens according to the law of cause and effect. There is a cause behind everything. We do not see the causes operating in a given instance; so we attribute it to "chance," "coincident," or "accident," or things of that nature.

Charles R. was afraid that he was losing his vision. He went to an ophthalmologist, and learned that he did not have cataracts or glaucoma or any of the usual symptoms leading to blindness. Further tests found no medical evidence of incipient blindness, yet in fact his vision was slowly, but surely dimming. The medical profession today understands that psychic factors play a definite role in all disease. Disease is the lack of peace, lack of equilibrium, lack of serenity. It's impossible to have a healthy mind and a sick body.

A healthy mind is a healthy body. Nothing happens in the body except the equivalent is in the mind. There is no doubt that visual problems can be brought on by workings of the mind. Emotional reactions can cause the involuntary muscles to twist the eyeball out of shape. Treating the mental and emotional factors of the individual rather than just concentrating on the eyes may reveal the basic emotional factor, the reason why the subconscious mind is selecting an ailment that tends to shut out everything except the immediate surroundings.

In my conversations with Charles he constantly complained about his mother-in-law who was living in his home. He vehemently stated; "I can't stand the sight of that woman." He was full of suppressed rage. His emotional system, which could not stand the strain any longer, selected the eyes as a scapegoat. The explanation was the cure in this case. He was surprised to learn that negative emotions, if persisted in, snarl up in the subconscious mind; and, being negative, must have a negative outlet.

The commands to his subconscious mind were negative: "I hate the sight of her. I don't want to see her any more." I explained to him: Your subconscious mind takes you literally. His statements were accepted by his subconscious mind; and the subconscious looked upon that as a request and proceeded to bring on loss of vision.

He and his wife agreed that it would be best if his mother-in-law lived elsewhere. They arranged for her to move to a senior citizen facility not too far away. However, moving her to another residence alone would not solve the problem entirely. Charles had to erase his hatred of his mother-in-law from his mind. At my suggestion he prayed for her by releasing her to God and wishing for her all the blessings of heaven. He did it in a very simple way. He said: "I surrender my mother-in-law (mentioning her name) to God completely. I radiate love, peace and goodwill to her. I wish for her all the blessings of heaven. I mean this. I'm sincere. I decree it. It shall all come to pass, and the light of God shall shine upon her ways."

As he continued to do that, I explained to him that he would know when he had completely accepted her, because he could meet her in his mind and there would be no sting there. He would no longer sizzle. His vision began to improve almost immediately, and soon his eyesight was restored to normal. The ophthalmologist looked at his eyes and said: "You solved your problem"; and he *had* solved his problem. He could meet her in his mind and there was no sting there. He no longer sizzled.

In the beginning of this chapter, we brought out that you should concentrate your thoughts on whatsoever things are true, lovely, noble, and Godlike. Think on these things, because you are what you think all day long. And our life is what our thoughts have made it. You don't want the irrational mass mind thinking in you, do you? No, you don't. If you do not think for yourself, you must ask yourself who is manipulating your mind now. Ask yourself: Do I own my own mind? Do I come to my own decisions? Am I thinking clearly, according to Godlike patterns?

You cannot dodge or circumvent the law of mind. It is done unto you, as you believe. Years ago the English sailors blamed scurvy on the salt meat they had—hardtack and so on. Then someone told them to eat some limes, some lemons, full of Vitamin C; and, of course, they were healed. But, you see, again, that was ignorance, carelessness, indifference, stupidity. It was a void in the mind. Because all the islands and all the countries they visited in their long voyages were full of oranges, apples, limes, lemons, and all kinds of citrus fruits. Where was the lack? The lack was in the mind, a void in the mind, ignorance. Ignorance is no excuse for the law. It was carelessness, indifference and apathy. People are constantly attributing their ailments to the atmosphere, the weather, to malpractice, evil entities, germs, viruses and diets.

Most of us have no doubt that an invisible virus can make us ill, but we don't always believe in the Invisible Presence and Power called God, Which created us, and created the whole world.

We pollute the air with strange notions and false doctrines. If we believe that by nearing an electric fan we can catch cold or get a stiff neck, that belief, when accepted, becomes our master and ruler and causes us to experience a cold. Millions of people sit under fans all over the world; they don't get a stiff neck, they don't get a cold. Millions of people go out in the night air. They don't get a chill or pneumonia ever. Millions of people get their feet wet. But maybe your mother said when you get your feet wet and you don't dry them and put on new socks you'll get your death of cold, or pneumonia, or something. But the water never said: "I'll give you pneumonia, a chill, a fever, or anything."

According to your belief it is done unto you. According to your faith it is done unto you. Your faith should be in the goodness of God in the land of the living, and the guidance of God, and the Healing Power of God, the abundance of God, and in the fact that an Infinite Intelligence responds to you when you call upon it.

The fan is harmless. It's mechanical; it's innocuous. Your faith can be used two ways. You can have faith in an invisible virus to give you the flu, or you can have faith in the invisible Spirit within you to flow through you as harmony, health, peace, guidance and right action, as a God, or Spirit, in you cannot be sick, and the Spirit in you is God. What is true of God is true of you, because the word *individual* means the Indivisible One. That's the Living Spirit Almighty within you. The Bible says: "I said ye are Gods, and all of you are children of the Most High." Believe that you are a child of the Living God. You are. Believe that the Living Spirit within you is the God Presence, and that can't be sick. And because that can't be sick, that's the reality of you.

Emerson said we (humans) think our fate is alien, because the cause is hidden. But the soul (the subconscious mind) contains the event that shall befall it, for the event is only the actualization of its thoughts. What we pray to ourselves for is always granted.

The devil in the Bible means ignorance or misunderstanding. It means a false concept of God, life and the universe. The devil means ignorance or misunderstanding, misapplication of law. Actually, it means God upside down; a twisted, morbid, diabolical concept of the God of love. There's no being with hooves, horns and a tail. This comes out of our distorted, twisted imagination. Not willing to admit that the evil is within ourselves, we postulate it outside ourselves. Surely, God is omnipresent. Omnipresent means it must be present in you; otherwise, the word omnipresent has no meaning.

A man told me, for example, that he was wounded in the jungle, and he was praying that someone would come and rescue him. And he said: "There was a man who was hunting in that jungle and had a sudden feeling that he should change his course. He did so and came and administered to my wound and helped me back to a home." The man who was wounded was praying for help, and this man who was out hunting changed his course. He had an intuitive feeling, perception. It was the Infinite Intelligence guiding the hunter to become his rescuer. But it was the One Being operating in both.

It is done unto you as you believe, and a belief is a thought in the mind. No external power or evil entity is trying to lure or harm you. People are constantly attributing their ailments to the atmosphere, the weather, and some attribute their trouble to the voodoo. They say it's black magic, or "Someone is practicing voodoo against me." No person has any power. The Power of God is in you. One with God is a majority. If God be for you, who can be against you?

Spell *live* backwards; you have *evil*. That's living life backwards. Then you have your evil. Your evil is the inversion of the Life Principle, Which is God. God moves as Unity; seeks to express Himself through you as beauty, love, joy, peace and Divine order. The will of God for you is a greater measure of life, love, truth and beauty, something transcending your fondest dreams.

Realize, therefore, that God is guiding you, that there is right action in your life. Read and meditate on the 91st Psalm, (see chapter 6) and realize that you dwell in the secret place of the Most High, that you abide in the shadow of the Almighty. You'll say of the Lord: *He is my refuge and my fortress; my God, in Him will I trust. He covers me with His feathers; under His wings shall I trust.* Just like the hen gathers the chickens together to protect them, so does that Heavenly Father in you surround you with the invisible arm of God's love, rendering you impervious to all harm. You become immunized; you become God-intoxicated, because you've received the Divine antibody.

The false idea in your mind is called the adversary, the devil, Satan, and so on. The devils that bedevil us are enmity, strife, hatred; they are devils created by ourselves. They drive some people insane. Because if you put gangsters in charge of your mind, what do you expect? If you fail to believe in the goodness of God and a God of love, the extent to which you believe this can well be your so-called devil, which is the source of your pains, aches and misfortune.

God, or the Living Spirit Almighty, or the Life Principle, doesn't judge or punish; it can't. Good and evil are the movements of one's own mind. It is very primitive thinking to believe that God is punishing us or that a devil is tempting us.

Our state of consciousness is always made manifest. That's the way you think, believe, and feel whatever you give mental consent to. There is no other cause in the world. Men, women and children are constantly testifying to our state of mind, to our mental attitudes, to our convictions, to our beliefs.

We must remember that the majority of people do not discipline, control or direct their thinking and mental imagery along Godlike channels. Therefore, their failure to think constructively and harmoniously from the standpoint of the Infinite One means that they leave their minds open to the irrational mass mind, which is full of fears, hates, jealousy, and all kinds of negative happenings and destructive thinking of all kinds.

There is a story of a man who had been fired from his job by a cruel and mean boss. He made up his mind to shoot him. Every day he waited behind a shed near the factory for the boss to pass by. To avoid being caught, he planned to wait for a time when nobody else was near.

He had a rifle. On the third morning, when he was stealthily moving into the shed, he stumbled, the rifle went off, and a bullet pierced his heart. He killed himself.

People call that an accident. That was no accident; He had murder in his heart; and murder is of the heart. In the Ten Commandments we are told, "Thou shall do no murder." It doesn't say, "Thou shalt not kill." That is a commonly held belief because of an early mistranslation of the original Hebrew. When you read the original, it says: "Thou shall do no murder." Then it tells you that murder is of the heart.

When you hate, and when you resent, and you are full of hostility and resentment. Then you are murdering love, peace, harmony, discernment, kindness and everything that's good. And as you continue to hate and resent, these reach a point of saturation in your subconscious mind and are precipitated as cancer, a bullet, a fatal accident or something else. But that negative, destructive emotion must have an outlet; and sooner or later reaches a point of saturation and is precipitated on the screen of space. There are no accidents. There's a mind, a mood, a feeling behind a car, train, bicycle, and also behind the gun. A gun is harmless—it is just a piece of metal. It doesn't do any harm to anybody. It's the mind behind it. You can kill with a stone, kill with poison, with a club, a thousand and one ways. But the stone is harmless; the club is harmless. How do you use it? This man had murder in his heart for a long time, and his subconscious responded accordingly.

The Bible tells you: "No manifestation cometh unto me save I, the Father, draw it." And the father of all is your thought and feeling. It fathers everything. The union of your conscious and subconscious mind, your thought and feeling, is the cause of your destiny. That's the cause of every single thing in your world. Whatever your conscious and subconscious minds agree on comes to pass. Any idea emotionalized and felt as true must come to pass.

The Father is your state of consciousness, your own creative power which brings all things to pass in your world. No experience comes to you unless there is an affinity in your own mind. Two unlike things repel each other. Harmony and discord do not dwell together. Therefore, if you believe the whole armor of God surrounds you, enfolds you and enwraps you; and the harmonizing, healing power of God takes care of you, you can't be on a train that gets wrecked; you can't be on a plane that catches on fire or where someone planted a bomb. If you walk and talk with God and believe that God is guiding you, and that the law of harmony is always governing you, then you cannot be on a train that is wrecked because, as we said, discord and harmony do not dwell together.

It would be naïve to assume that changing one's beliefs from negative to positive could cure all illnesses and disabilities. There are, indeed, organic and physical causes for most ailments. However, there is a significant portion of health problems that are psychosomatic. It is these that thought-change can reverse. I have heard about examples of this in many countries and over many time periods and I have been instrumental in helping many people by providing them with prayers and meditations to help program their subconscious minds to bring them back to health.

Guilt, worry and fear are the psychosomatic equivalent of germs and viruses. By replacing thoughts of guilt, worry and fear with thoughts of faith, confidence and belief, healing is accelerated.

Most cases are not at all dramatic. They may take the form of insomnia, allergies, headaches, digestive disorders or depression. In other cases they may be major maladies such as tumors, paralysis, ulcers, coronary disease or psychological breakdowns.

When afflicted, we tend to blame others. It may be another person. "I've been cursed by an enemy," It may be your family history. "I come from a weak genetic background." It may be divine retribution. "I'm being punished by God."

As shown earlier in this chapter, the real cause lies within you. It is you and only you who have control of your thoughts. Others may influence you, but it is you and only you who can make the decision on what will be accepted by your conscious mind and seep down into your subconscious.

Let us cease blaming others. Let us look within for the cause of all. Believe in God, believe in the goodness of God, believe in the love of God and God's guidance; and you will find that all your ways will be those of pleasantness and all your paths will be paths of peace. Because you are belief expressed.

People ask me about children. They say children don't know how to pray; and some children are caught in a fire, drowned at sea on a ship, and things of that nature. Well, children are under the watchful eyes of their parents. And God gave love to all fathers and all mothers, the lion and the lioness, too, to all animals. God's love dwells within the father and mother; and it is their mission to cause that child to grow in the image and the likeness of the Divine Presence of God. They are there to realize that the child grows up in the image and the likeness of the dominant mental and emotional climate of the home.

The child cannot yet discern and reason; therefore, the parents mold the consciousness of the child. A child is subject to the atmosphere of the home. Therefore, you realize that the child is God's child and God's love fills its soul; it's growing in wisdom, truth and beauty. God planted His love in fathers and mothers that they might lead their children through the darkness of the night and through the vicissitudes of life into a realization of God's Holy Presence, and to teach him of the God of Love, and that the love of God is flowing through them in transcendent loveliness, and that He careth for them. And children brought up to believe that God is love, and His love enfolds them, surrounds them and enwraps them, will grow in a magnificent way; and God will be with them all the days of their life.

In a Nutshell

When your thoughts are completely free from fear and worry, you are thinking from the standpoint of the Divine center within you; and God speaks, thinks and acts through you. Therefore, you speak in words of wisdom, truth and beauty; words of harmony, health and peace. You think, therefore, from the God center within.

If you do not think constructively, harmoniously and peacefully, the mass mind will do your thinking for you. And that mass mind believes in tragedy, misfortune, sickness, disease, accidents; hate, murder, and all sorts of things. If you don't do your own thinking, these negative vibrations, or thoughts of the mass mind, move in upon you, reach a point of saturation, precipitate as accident, misfortune, sickness, disease.

The law of life is the law of belief. If you fear sickness, you attract it. If you think good health, you will be healthy. The law of the Lord is perfect. You can't think one thing and produce another. Trouble of any kind is nature's alarm system that we are thinking wrongly in that direction. Nothing but a change of thought can set us free.

There is no worse suffering than a guilty conscience, and, certainly, none more destructive. Stop condemning yourself and begin to accept that the Infinite healing presence saturates your whole being, that God dwells in every cell of your body.

It is done unto you as you believe, and a belief is a thought in the mind. No external power or evil entity is trying to lure or harm you. No person has any power. The Power of God is in you. One with God is a majority. If God be for you, who can be against you?

Guilt, worry and fear are the psychosomatic equivalent of germs and viruses. By replacing thoughts of guilt, worry and fear with thoughts of faith, confidence and belief, healing is accelerated.

CHAPTER EIGHT

Prayer Is the Key

Are you consumed with fear or worry? From time to time all people face problems that cause such concern that they dominate their lives. Some of these are unfounded. We worry about things that are unlikely to occur or are figments of our imagination. But often the problems are true and imminent. We worry about debts we cannot pay; we worry about our health or the health of a loved one. We worry about our jobs or our investments.

The first step in overcoming these worries is to take pragmatic steps by working to correct the problem. But in addition we must program our minds so that we will have the confidence to work through the problems and restore and maintain a positive outlook on life.

There is one way, one key to accomplishing this. It is by prayer and meditation.

What is prayer? Your every thought and feeling is your prayer. Every thought tends to manifest itself unless it is neutralized by a thought of greater intensity. In the specific sense, prayer is conscious contact with the Infinite Intelligence within you. Effective prayer must be based upon the spiritual premise that there is a Supreme Intelligence within us that becomes the thing we desire. To the degree that we accept this as being true. Effective prayer is a sustained, affirmative attitude of mind that results in conviction. Once your desire is completely accepted subconsciously, it works automatically as part of the creative law.

The real test of whether or not you have reached a conviction is that your mind accepts the idea completely and cannot conceive of the opposite. You must believe what you want to believe. When you do, you have really impressed your subconscious mind; then your subconscious will respond accordingly.

There is an Infinite Intelligence operating in your subconscious mind that responds to your conscious mind's thinking and imagining. You must come to a definite decision in your conscious mind. You must decide what you want to know, and then trust the deeper mind to answer you. When you turn over your request to your subconscious mind, you should do so with the absolute conviction that it has the know-how of accomplishment and that it will respond to you according to the nature of your request.

The Bible says: "Ask and it shall be given you; seek and ye shall find; knock and it shall be opened unto you. For everyone that asketh, receiveth; he that seeketh, findeth; to him that knocketh, it shall be opened. What man is there of you whom, if his son asks bread, will he give him a stone? Or if he asks fish, will he give him a serpent?"

Here the Bible tells you that when you ask for bread, you will not get a stone; but, rather, the embodiment of your request. Keep on asking, seeking and knocking until you receive a response from your subconscious mind, the nature of which is responsiveness. Become enthusiastic. Feel and know that there is a solution to every problem, a way out of every dilemma, that there are no incurable conditions. There are people who believe they are incurable; and, of course, it is done unto them as they believe. But, with God all things are possible.

We all seek serenity in our lives. Serenity is our strength in God, the healing, protective Presence within and around us. Serenity is the higher awareness of the Presence of God that enables us to remain utterly calm and poised, regardless of the turmoil, turbulence, and the confusion that is rampant in the world around us.

Serenity is an attribute of God's Presence, a gift achieved, within the reach and grasp of all of us. It is our refuge and our fortress in times of trouble, of the constant change. When we look to the outer, or world, conditions for stability and sustenance, we look in vain. The outer world is in a constant state of vanity or change.

Our worries and fears destroy our serenity. It can be restored if we pray effectively. To pray effectively, you change your mind to conform to the eternal verities, which never change. You do not beg, supplicate or beseech. To do so is to attract more lack and limitation, because you are denying that it is already given to you, for God is the giver and the gift. No matter what you seek already is because everything comes forth from the Infinite. You simply reorder your mind and align yourself with the truth.

When the Nazi army marched into Vienna in March of 1938, Vicki W. faced a major crisis. Although she was Catholic, she had recently married a Jew. The Nazis declared all marriages between Jews and Gentiles void. Her family pleaded with her to accept the Nazi-ordained annulment and return to them. Her husband, fearful that she would share his fate, urged her to do the same. He said, "I don't know what will happen to me. You will be better off if you leave me."

Vicki prayed. "I love my husband. I want to stay with him, to raise a family with him, and I know the dangers. We may be forcibly separated, sent to concentration camps, even killed. Please God, give me the strength and wisdom to make the right decision."

She said this prayer each morning at church and again each evening at home. She refused to leave. Meanwhile her husband put all of his efforts in attempting to find a way to leave Austria. They were frustrated over and over again, but her prayers kept them from losing hope.

After working through the bureaucratic red tape, and with the help of her husband's relatives in the United States, they obtained visas to come to America. They left Austria just weeks before the Nazis clamped down on Jews trying to emigrate.

Vicki and her husband settled in Los Angeles, survived his service in the U.S. Army during the ensuing war and raised a fine family. Prayer helped her through this and other crises in her life.

Most people do not have to face such life-threatening crises, but worry about their day-to-day problems. A common source of worry is discord in your home or on your job. Prayer can help. You can claim that the absolute harmony of the Infinite One reigns supreme in your mind and in that of the other person or persons. This prayer of the absolute harmony of the Infinite animating, sustaining and permeating the entire atmosphere will bring results. Re-arrange all your thoughts, imagery and responses on the side of peace and harmony. If you see hatred in the other, practice knowing that Divine love dissolves everything unlike Itself in the mind and heart of that person and also in your own mind and heart. This would be effective prayer.

What is true of the Infinite is true of you. To know this is the truth that sets you free. If you do not know the answer to a perplexing problem, claim that the wisdom of the Infinite reveals to you the answer. You will receive it. God is the name for that Infinite Presence and Power within you, for the Principle of life and for the way your conscious and subconscious mind works. Where divine love, peace, harmony and joy live, there is no evil, harm or sickness.

The cure for all your problems is to practice the Presence of God, which means to fill your soul with Divine love, Divine peace and Divine power, and Divine harmony, and Divine right action. If you believe in sickness, disease and failure, you will always get the reaction of your own belief. The great truths of the Infinite are available to all just the same as the sun shines on the just and the unjust, and the rain falls on the good and the evil. All that is necessary is faith in God. Faith in its true meaning is the practice of the Presence of God.

From earliest times, people have asked why do we have wars, famines, disasters, and ill health? These are given to us that we might mature within ourselves to the achieved state of serenity to be found within ourselves. All the problems and vicissitudes and vexations we experience are to cause us to wake up and to become mature.

They are not bad or evil in the intent in themselves. It is the veil of spiritual ignorance, the darkness of not knowing, which prevents us from seeing or perceiving or failing to discover our own powers of goodness and love and light, that cause our suffering.

Problems of life are not in existing conditions or circumstances, but in the person of man and woman. This idea is not popular with those who desire to hear only how mistreated and abused they are, but to those who want to heal themselves and their lives, it is the Presence within us which ever says: "You are greater than you may know now!"

Because of this Presence, this attitude and life tendency, we continue to seek, rather than to sit back and attempt nothing. It is the belief and philosophy of the majority to claim, "Society, the world, or my parents and family, are responsible for my misery and unhappiness." This is not true. The wisdom of the Presence within says: "You are responsible for triumph and achievement. You have aspired to higher understand, you know better way!"

One of our greatest and most liberating triumphs is the knowledge and wisdom that there are certain things we cannot change, and it is not needful for us to want to! "God, grant us the wisdom to know the difference!"

All that is required and asked of you is that you change in perception and conviction. That every one has God-given privilege to be as he or she is. Let them go to find their highest good in God. The weight of the world will fall from your shoulders! You are not responsible for the world. Heal yourself; disabuse yourself that you are responsible for ills and evils of world.

Allow everyone, including your children, to find themselves. You have done your best to give them sense of ethics, morality—no one can do more than that. Let them go; release them to God. Heal yourself of the messianic complex and perception that you are responsible for everything. You are not! We cannot save the world.

You are responsible for yourself. Change yourself and your world (the world) with change for the better. This contributes to good of world, of humankind. That is your responsibility. The alternative is to wait for the entire world to change. Why weary and exhaust yourself further? What has it accomplished?

Serenity is spiritual maturity. It is achieved following the realization that God, the Father within and of all, is in charge of the universe and the world. "Father within doeth the works." Take charge of yourself, yourself only, this and this alone gives birth to serenity in the face of change. It may sound callous to state these ideas. It is not. It is pragmatic and effective.

Some years ago I listened to a sales manager talk to his staff. He said, "The first thing you do is to find a prospect. The second step is to get that person's attention and interest. The third step is to win his or her confidence and create a desire. The fourth step is to know that it is done, which closes the sale." This process that leads to a successful sale can also be applied to successful prayer.

Are you sold on the Infinite? Do you believe implicitly that God, the Infinite Intelligence in you, can heal you? That's your prospect. This is your first step in making prayer work for you. It can solve your problem, wipe away all tears, set you on the high road to happiness, freedom and peace of mind. The second step is to get the attention and interest. If you believe implicitly that there is a Healing Presence within you, you are selling yourself to your Higher Self. Your Higher Self is your prospect. Give your attention to the Infinite and Divine love. Believe that God, Who made you, can heal you. Be sincere and honest. Give all power and allegiance to the Infinite. You must give allegiance and recognition to no other power. Then and only then are you selling yourself to the Infinite.

Begin to use your mind in the right way. Refuse to give power to anything but the Living Spirit Almighty within you. Then you eliminate from your mind false beliefs and touch the Presence of the Infinite, resulting in an instantaneous healing.

In other words, the first step in praying effectively is complete allegiance, devotion and loyalty to the Only Presence and Power within you. This Power created you. It can heal you. Secondly, you must definitely, absolutely and completely refuse to give power to any external thing or any other power but the Infinite. You give no power to the phenomenalistic world, or to any person, place or thing. The third step: Whatever the problem, difficulty or sickness may be, turn away from the problem and affirm feelingly and knowingly: "God is, and this Infinite Healing Presence flows through me now, vitalizing, energizing, and healing my whole being. Infinite love flows through me as right action and Divine freedom."

The fourth step is to give thanks for the happy solution. Rejoice and say: "Father, I thank Thee for the perfect answer. I know it is God in action now. I have mentally touched the border of His garment, and I have pinpointed the whole reaction of the Infinite Power. It is wonderful."

But turn to the Divine Presence and remind yourself of that Infinite ocean of peace, of absolute harmony, wholeness, beauty, boundless love and limitless power. Know that the Infinite Presence and Power loves you and cares for you. As you pray this way, fear will gradually fade away. Turn your mind to God and His love. Feel and know that there is only One Healing Power and Its corollary. There is no power to challenge the action of the Infinite.

Quietly and lovingly affirm that the uplifting, healing, strengthening power of the Healing Presence is flowing through you, making you every whit whole. Know and feel that the harmony, beauty and life of the Infinite are made manifest in you as strength, as peace, as vitality, as beauty, wholeness and right action.

If you pray about a heart condition, do not think of the organ that is diseased. This would not be spiritual thinking. Thoughts are things. Your spiritual thought takes the form of cells, tissue, nerves and organs. To think of a damaged heart or high blood pressure tends to suggest more of what you already have. Cease dwelling on symptoms, organs or any part of the body. Simply dwell upon the Infinite Healing Presence within you, flowing through you as beauty, love, harmony, joy, wisdom, power, and strength. Then you are really glorifying God in your body.

Live joyously in the world, but do not succumb and eat and drink of its ills and travails. Extract every sense of joy and pleasure within it; don't leave half undone. Providence, love, protection of God are all around. Open your eyes to see them and your heart to receive them. You will know and love the heart fulfilled and made serene, it is the unchanging, eternal love of God.

In a Nutshell

Your every thought and feeling is your prayer. Every thought tends to manifest itself unless it is neutralized by a thought of greater intensity. In the specific sense, prayer is conscious contact with the Infinite Intelligence within you. Effective prayer must be based upon the spiritual premise that there is a Supreme Intelligence within us that becomes the thing we desire.

There is an Infinite Intelligence operating in your subconscious mind that responds to your conscious mind's thinking and imagining. When you turn over your request to your subconscious mind, you should do so with the absolute conviction that it has the know-how of accomplishment that it will respond to you according to the nature of your request.

If you are having discord with another person, rearrange all your thoughts, imagery and responses on the side of peace and harmony. If you see hatred in the other, practice knowing that Divine love dissolves everything unlike Itself in the mind and heart of that person and also in your own mind and heart.

All that is required and asked of you is that you change in perception and conviction that every one has God-given privilege to be as he or she is. Let them go to find their highest good in God. The weight of the world will fall from your shoulders! You are not responsible for the world. Heal yourself; disabuse yourself that you are responsible for ills and evils of world.

Know that the Infinite Presence and Power loves you and cares for you. As you pray this way, fear will gradually fade away. Turn your mind to God and His love. Feel and know that there is only One Healing Power and Its corollary. There is no power to challenge the action of the Infinite.

CHAPTER NINE

Sleep Soundly

You spend about eight out of every twenty-four hours, or one-third of your life, in sleep. Sleep is a Divine law. Many answers to our problems come to us when we are sound asleep. Many people have advocated the theory that you get tired during the day and you go to sleep to rest the body, and a repairing process takes place while you sleep. Nothing rests in sleep. He who watches over all of us neither slumbers nor sleeps. Your heart, lungs and all your vital organs function while you are asleep. If you eat prior to sleep, the food is digested and assimilated. Also, your skin secretes perspiration; your nails continue to grow.

Your body is repaired; new cells grow to replace worn out ones, nerves and organs revitalize themselves. Most important, your subconscious mind never rests or sleeps.

It is always active, controlling all your vital forces. In sleep, the conscious mind is creatively joined to the subconscious.

Go to sleep every night with the praise of God forever on your lips. The healing process takes place more rapidly while you are asleep, as there is no interference from your conscious mind. Quite often answers to the problems that have been on your mind all day are given to you while you are asleep. Scientific research on sleep has demonstrated that at night, while asleep, you receive impressions showing that the nerves of the eyes, ears, nose and taste buds are active during sleep. Also, the nerves of your brain are quite active.

These studies show that the supposed exemption from customary toils and activities was not the final purpose of sleep but that no part of a person's life deserves to be considered more indispensable to its symmetrical and perfect spiritual development than when one is asleep.

Lack of sleep causes you to become irritable, moody and depressed. It is generally accepted that all human beings need a minimum of six hours of sleep to be healthy. Most people need more.

Medical research scholars investigating sleep processes and deprivation of sleep point out that severe insomnia has preceded psychotic breakdown in some instances. Remember, you are spiritually recharged during sleep, and adequate sleep is essential to produce joy and vitality in life.

Experiments about sleep have been in progress for many years. Subjects have been kept awake for as long as four days. Thousands of tests have measured the effects of their behavior and personality. Results of these tests have given scientists astonishing new insights into the mysteries of sleep. They now know that the tired brain apparently craves sleep so hungrily that it will sacrifice anything to get it. After only a few hours of sleep loss, fleeting stolen naps called *lapses* or microsleep occurred at the rate of three or four an hour. As in real sleep, eyelids drooped, the heartbeat slowed. Each lapse lasted just a fraction of a second. Sometimes the lapses were periods of blackness; sometimes they were filled with images, wisps of dreams.

As hours of sleep loss mounted, the lapses took place more often and lasted longer—perhaps two or three seconds. Even if the subjects had been piloting an airliner in a thunderstorm, they still couldn't have resisted microsleeps for these few priceless seconds. It can happen to you, as many of you who have fallen asleep at the wheel of a car can testify.

Another startling effect of sleep deprivation was its attack on human memory and perception. Many sleep-deprived subjects were unable to retain information long enough to relate it to the tasks they were supposed to perform. They were totally befuddled in situations requiring them to hold several factors in mind and act on them, as a pilot must when he skillfully integrates wind direction, air speed, altitude, and glide path to make a safe landing.

The opportunity offered George G. seemed fantastic. A former co-worker was starting a new company to tie in with the rapidly growing Internet industry, commonly referred to as the "dot-com" boom. He was a brilliant engineer and George had great confidence in his technical skills. The investment required was $50,000—practically all the money George had in his portfolio. He pondered over whether to accept or not. Success would make him a millionaire, but failure would wipe him out.

Prior to going to sleep the night before the decision had to be made, he prayed as follows:

The Creative Intelligence of my subconscious mind knows what is best for me. Its tendency is always lifeward and reveals to me the right decision, which blesses me and all concerned. I give thanks for the answer, which I know will come to me.

George repeated this simple prayer over and over again as a lullaby prior to sleep. In the morning he had a persistent feeling that he should not make the investment. He still had reservations. The temptation to take the risk was great, but he chose to follow his feelings and declined the offer. He watched the company start up and begin to flourish, but only a few months later the entire "dot-com" boom burst and this company collapsed with it.

The conscious mind may be correct on the facts objectively known, but the intuitive faculty of the subconscious mind saw the failure of the concern in question and guided him to the right decision.

If you suffer from insomnia or you have difficulty in sleep, just dwell upon these wonderful words from the Psalms. In the Fourth Psalm it says: "I lay me down in peace to sleep, for Thou, Lord, maketh me dwell in safety." And the 127th Psalm says: "For so He giveth His beloved in sleep, for He Who watches over Israel neither slumbers nor sleeps." In the Book of Proverbs it says: "I lay me down in peace to sleep, for Thou, Lord, maketh me dwell in safety." "Thy sleep shall be sweet. I will lay me down in peace and sleep, for Thou, Lord, maketh me dwell in safety." Repeat that to yourself frequently and you will be amazed what a wonderful sleep you will have. "I will lay me down in peace to sleep, for Thou, Lord, maketh me dwell in safety."

Quietly repeat that to yourself. You will be amazed what a wonderful, peaceful sleep you have. Proverbs says: "Yet a little sleep, a little slumber, a little folding, and Thy hands to sleep."

As you sleep, you feel you are now what you long to be. Relax and let go. And what you are seeking is your desire, the ideal, and the thing closest to your heart. Realize that

God gave you that desire. Say, "I go off to sleep and I completely accept it, and I walk in the light that it is so."

Accept the reality of your desire as you go to sleep. Assume the feeling of being what you long to be. Assume that you now have what you long to possess. Assume you are now experiencing that which you long to be. And live in that role. Live in that mood. You go off into the deep of sleep, and you are impregnating your subconscious mind.

Sleep is a state of oneness, and if you repeat *peace* to yourself, "peace, peace, peace," you will go off sleep, too. Or you repeat one word, *sleep* to lull yourself to sleep. "Sleep, sleep, sleep." Just one word. Silently say it to yourself, and you will go off into the deep of sleep.

Remember, that the future, the result of your habitual thinking, is already in your mind except when you change it through prayer. The future of the country is in the collective subconscious of the people of that nation. Realize that marvelous answers sometimes come to you in sleep. You are building your future now by your habitual thinking and your imagery. Every night of your life, when you close your eyes, if you have difficulties, as I said, sleeping, say, "I sleep in peace, I wake in joy, I live in God." Or, "I sleep for eight hours in peace, I wake in joy, I live in God." Then take one word, "peace," and lull yourself to sleep with that one word. Sleep is a state of oneness. Or you can just say to yourself, "Sleep, sleep."

The following prayer helps give confidence, peace and comfort. Repeat it each night when you lie down:

Eternal God, grant that we may lie down in peace and raise us up to life renewed. Spread over us the shelter of Your peace; guide us with Your good counsel; and for Your name's sake, be our help.

Shield us from hatred and plague; keep us from war and famine and anguish; subdue our inclinations to evil, O God, our guardian and helper; our gracious and merciful ruler, give us refuge in the shadow of your wings. O guard our coming and going, that now and always we have life and Peace.

In my book *The Power of Your Subconscious Mind*, I tell the story of how a marvelous answer was given to a man while he was two minutes asleep. His name was Ray Hammerstrong, a worker in a steel mill in Pennsylvania. A faulty switch in a newly installed bar mill that controlled the delivery of straight bars to the cooling beds was not working properly and held up production. The engineers worked on the switch but could not solve the problem.

Hammerstrong thought a lot about the problem and tried to figure out a new design that might work. Nothing worked. One afternoon he lay down to sleep to take a nap. Prior to sleep, he began to think about the answer to the switch problem. He had a dream while he was sound asleep in which a perfect design for the switch was portrayed. When he awoke he sketched his new design according to the outline in his dream. His visionary catnap won Hammerstrong a check for $15,000, the largest award the firm had ever given an employee for a new idea.

Yes, often you are instructed in your sleep, the way out, the solution to your problem. So is the scientist, so is the chemist. You are the master of your thoughts, emotions and responses to life. When you pray, become a good executive. Learn to delegate and turn over your request to your subconscious mind with faith and confidence. The deeper mind knows how to solve your problem and presents you with the answer.

Turn your request over now with faith and confidence. Know in your heart you will have actually turned over your request to the deeper mind full of wisdom and intelligence. You will receive an answer, for it is written: "In quietness and in confidence shall be your strength."

Never go to sleep with negative thoughts in your mind. It is of the utmost importance to make yourself feel strong and optimistic at night; to erase all signs, convictions, and feelings of uncertainty and fear; to throw aside every care and worry that would carve its image on your brain and express itself in your face. The worrying mind actually generates calcareous matter in the brain and hardens the cells.

You should fall asleep holding those desires and ideals uppermost in the mind which are dearest to you; which you are the most anxious to realize. As the mind continues to work during sleep, these desires and ideals are thus intensified and increased. It is well known that impure thoughts and desires work terrible havoc then. Purity of thought, loftiness of purpose, the highest possible aims, should dominate the mind when you fall asleep.

When you first wake in the morning, picture the positive qualities as vividly possible. Say to yourself: "I am well and healthy, strong and buoyant. I will succeed in my goals, will be healthy in body and sound in mind because in the truth of my being I am divine, and Divine Principle cannot be defeated."

Remember this great prayer: "I sleep in peace, I wake in joy, I live in God now and forever more."

In a Nutshell

Quite often answers to the problems that have been on your mind all day are given to you while you are asleep.

Remember, you are spiritually recharged during sleep, and adequate sleep is essential to produce joy and vitality in life.

Assume the feeling of being what you long to be. Assume that you now have what you long to possess. Assume you are now experiencing that which you long to be. And live in that role. Live in that mood. You go off into the deep of sleep, and you are impregnating your subconscious mind.

Often you are instructed in your sleep, the way out, the solution to your problem. You are the master of your thoughts, emotions and responses to life. When you pray, delegate and turn over your request to your subconscious mind with faith and confidence. The deeper mind knows how to solve your problem and presents you with the answer. You will receive an answer, for it is written: "In quietness and in confidence shall be your strength."

CHAPTER TEN

Living In the Presence

S o many people when faced with worry and fear turn to the Book of Psalms for comfort and guidance. All 150 psalms inspire us and help us in times of trouble and travail. In previous chapters I showed how Psalms 23 and 91 are especially suited to help us deal with life's problems. In this chapter I want to present another great psalm, number 139, sometimes called "the entire Bible in miniature." As it is a very long psalm, here is an abbreviated version covering its key points.

> *O Lord, thou has searched me and known me . . .*
> *Thou understandeth my thought, afar off.*
> *Thou knowest my path and art acquainted with all*
>   *my ways. For there is not a word in my tongue,*
>   *but lo, O Lord, thou knowest it altogether . . .*

Whither shall I go from thy spirit? Or whither shall I flee from they presence?

If I ascend up into heaven, thou art there. If I make my bed in hell, behold, thou art there.

If I take the wings of the morning and dwell in the uttermost parts of the sea,

Even there shall thy hand lead me and thy right hand shall hold me.

If I say, surely, the darkness shall cover me; even the right shall be light about me.

Yea, the darkness and the light are both alike to thee

For thou hast possessed my reins; thou hast covered me in my mother's womb.

I will praise thee; for I am fearfully and wonderfully made. Marvelous are thy works and that my soul knoweth right well.

My substance was not hid from thee, when I was made in secret and curiously wrought in the lowest parts of the Earth.

Thine eyes did see my substance, yet being imperfect and in thy book, all my members were written, which in continuance were fashioned, when as yet there was none of them . . .

Search me, O God and know my heart . . . And see if there be any wicked way in me and lead me in the way everlasting.

It is no wonder that this inspired prayer has been described as "The Crown of all the Psalms." In the symbology of the Judeo-Christian Bible, in nearly all Scriptures, the crown is representative of our Divinity, our innate, creative and royal nature.

Psychologically, it portrays and reveals our inherent, inborn ability and capability to transform, or correct, all that we consider wrongful in our circumstances, through the power of the Creative Presence within, everlastingly responding to the "thoughts of our mind, the meditations of our Heart" (by which we mean our deeper mind), the creative Presence of Lord God.

Ibn Ezra, a Jewish scholar of 10th Century, Toledo, Spain, termed Psalm 139 "The Crown of all Psalms." Ibn Ezra was a learned man, author of many books on mathematics, astronomy, medicine and philosophy (also a noted poet). He is best known for his Commentaries on the Bible. (Those of you who enjoy works of Robert Browning may recognize Ibn Ezra as the inspiration of Browning's "Rabbi Ben Ezra.")

Ibn Ezra deemed the Crown of Psalms to be so because it is an entire Bible (or book) in miniature. In some of the most inspired and exalted passages in Scripture some of the most soul-stirring, moving verses translated to English offers the four essentials to a greater awareness and appreciation of who we are and the realization of our role in life (and to realize that we must learn that there are four essential truth to be granted so that we can accept and wear the crown of understanding now, to experience a better life now, rather than to postpone it into an indefinite, vague and uncertain future.

It is learning to live in the present moment, to realize the Presence of a loving, intelligent God. Briefly stated, four essential truths are these:

- First, we must accept God as a Presence who is omnipresent and universal;
- Second, omnipresence, God, being everywhere, is within us. We are in it. God is love; our relationship is as a beloved one.
- Third, the Presence is Omniscient: God knows all and sees all and being love, forgives
- Fourth, the psalmist informs of a way to apply, use, these truths to heal, restore, and correct mind-body conditions and relationships.

Truly, Psalm 139 is the Bible in miniature. It poses the deepest, most penetrating question or query of the Old Testament. "Whither shall I go from they spirit, or whither shall I flee from they presence?" It suggests to us that the Creative Presence is far more than we may have been instructed and taught. To think of the Presence, filling all space and "all contained there" is, including ourselves, to expand our mind and extend or enlarge our most basic concepts and opinions of the very nature of Being, of God.

When the Psalmist stated, "If I ascend up into heaven, thou art there. If I make by bed in hell, behold, thou art there," was he speaking of a literal place in the skies somewhere or of a particular bed? Of course not. Modern interpreters of the bible no longer take the words literally. We know that the words are metaphors for deeper and deeper thoughts.

The Psalmist is talking about the omnipresence of God; and, being omnipresent, it must be in you. It is the very life of you. This Presence is always waiting for you to call up It. Regardless of the degree of bondage you may be in, this Presence and Power will respond as mercy, soothing, healing and restoring your soul.

The terms *heaven* and *hell* represent our states of consciousness. *Heaven* is the mind at peace. It is self-forgiveness. In Biblical symbology, "bed" suggests a state of rest, relaxation, when we're "asleep" the turbulence, confusion, strife of world. We see this all around. We're "resting in God," protected and secure as we claim these qualities of Omnipresence.

"Bed in hell" implies a state of immobility, inability to move forward or to achieve progress of any measurement or perception; the prayed of the heart unanswered. The bed is a not-so subtle reference to the creative act and principle of the power of our mind, beliefs, concepts, opinions and our emotions concerning them. It is the union, or marriage, of the masculine intellect and feminine emotions within us that create conditions, circumstances, and events. The marvel and the freedom we possess, is to know that we make this "bed."

The Psalmist is honest and responsible. He reveals his knowledge of and wisdom in the creative principle: "If I ascend," I, myself, accomplish, ascend in conscious awareness of the Omnipresence, I, myself, ascent into heaven of my mind at peace. (Our ultimate goal: at peace when we possess and achieve the tangible results and efforts of our prayers, our perceptions).

I, myself, have the same and identical freedom to "make my bed in hell." I, myself, create or cause the limited state in my personal world. In either event, the loving, intelligent, all-knowing Presence remains the same: always living, forever loving, everlastingly intelligent and caring for us.

At any moment, in every place, regardless of our present experience, the presence will create that which we think and feel to be true. Our current lives are testimony of this magnificent and unfailing principle and Presence. At any given moment, in every circumstance, we can and are urged to "Rise: Take up your bed and walk" forward in the Light of God's love and care for you.

The purpose and function of prayer, meditation, contemplation, is to cleanse the mind and to make the contents of the mind and heart obey our conscious direction. Literally, changing the habitual thought patterns and processes; make disciples of our mind and hearts. Contemplation equals to think with a pattern. It is difficult only for a little while, as we persist.

Soon, we find our responses changing to more constructive patterns. We respond (become responsible) more readily to healing and goodwill; more peaceful and congenial attitudes are formed. We respond more readily and intelligently to situation at hand. "If I ascend up into heaven; if I make bed in hell."

Reason within yourself, the life-transforming truths offered by the Psalmist. *I* is the symbol of the Presence within. *I* is the symbol of love, intelligence, wisdom. When Moses asked God his name, God responded, "I AM." It is not an accident that the Roman letter, "I," and Roman number, "I," are one and the same.

Observe what you say following the pronoun "I." You are announcing your concept of God and of yourself. Do not say—even to yourself—"I am poor; I am lonely; I am not good." If that is what how you feel about who you are, that is what you will be. Change those negative responses to positive ones. Say : "I AM good." "I AM healthy." "I AM blessed."

The Psalmist lays to rest the belief and approach to an anthropomorphic Deity—God in the image and likeness of a human, a superbeing, but nevertheless, a human. As a consequence, automatically, we enthrone in our consciousness a God outside and separate from ourselves. A whimsical, changeable being, meting out rewards and punishments according to an unfathomable plan or purpose.

It is this belief that is the primary cause of our problems. It appears we may be surrounded, engulfed by numerous, enormously difficult problems, never-ending ailments, and lack, limitations ("the bed we have made in hell") but if we are now as spiritually mature as Psalmist suggests, we realize and acknowledge we are really and actually repeating the same conditions, in a somewhat different guise.

We have been living, thinking, doing, apart and separate from our self. We separate ourselves from the source of all that can be imagined, the Holy or wholly one, universal creator of All, including ourselves. It is this sense of separation that gives birth to a feeling that we are lost—the lost soul.

How could we possibly be outside the Holy One? It is a mathematical impossibility. Two infinites would be a contradiction—They would cancel one another. It is a fundamental, conceptual premise of Life: "Hear, the Lord God is One."

All else is an elaboration and commentary on this Universal, greatest of all truths. Dare and have the heart or courage to believe and claim a loving, all-knowing God, which wants and desires you to know and receive far more than you know and desire to receive God.

Our relationship is reciprocal—it is mutual and it is good. Interesting to recall that in no fewer than 27 languages, the words, *good* and *God* are synonymous. Disabuse yourself of a punishing, reluctant, neglectful Presence, and you will begin an entirely new life-expression and experience.

A man who had read my book, *The Power of Your Subconscious Mind*, mentioned that it made good sense, but in applying the truths offered, he had lost his sense and feeling of God. There are no "accidents" in Divine Mind (a term used by early mystics for Omnipresent Intelligence). He hadn't merely "found the book." Obviously, he had been searching or seeking for higher understanding. He said further, "Now, I feel as though I have no God—only a cold, unfeeling principle."

What can be offered to one in this state of mind? I believe the kindest thing to offer is that this is a usual, "normal," transition. We do experience an interim or intermediate period. We're neither in heaven or hell. Rather a state of limbo—"Neither here nor there; fish nor fowl."

We seem unable either to swim in the great ocean of life or to soar, like the eagle, to higher realms. It is all right and understood in All-knowing Mind of the Infinite. Our purpose is not to undermine or ruin one's belief, but to offer higher understanding. "Not to destroy, but to fulfill the law."

The kindest, and I firmly believe, the wisest, suggestions to offer: Remain with your religion, observe and follow the dogma, rites, ritual; but continue to pray for wisdom, understanding, guidance. Continue to seek, for those who do, with patience and forbearance, do find.

You will soon discover that within Divine Mind are all aspects, characteristics and qualities of love, intelligence, patience and direction. And these heal the sense of separation from Source of our life and our longing. We know a loving and caring parent. These are restoring truths of Psalm 139. It is difficult, if not impossible, to separate thee truths in order to discuss and elaborate them. *O Lord, thou hast searched me and known me . . . thou understandeth my thought, afar off. Thou knowest my path . . . and art acquainted with all my ways . . . Search me, O God, and know my heart . . . And see if there be any wicked way in me and lead me in the way everlasting.*

If ever a word needs to be clarified, it is *wicked*. Far too many have been raised and told over and again they are intrinsically bad or wicked. This is a direct result and effect of misinterpretation of the Bible, of failing to remember we are reading a twice-translated document.

"Wicked" has come to signify an unhealthy, unwholesome attitude about and of ourselves, since the early years of the 12th Century, about the time the Bible was translated to English under the direction of King James. He delegated many qualified scholars—but the translation from one language to another, as I'm sure you know, always misses the mark of the original intent or concept.

The Hebrew-to-English lexicon defines *wicked* as any idea that causes sorrow or unhappiness. To be wicked equals to worry, to grieve one self, to offend or pain, to be angry. It is a term of mental discomfort. *Arise, take up your bed and walk.* To find you are in a state of hell, mental discomfort is a signal to redirect the attention, to identify with the good. "God in me knows how to correct this condition."

It is too much to think we must, even can, be perfect, without wickedness, without sin (erroneous use of faculties). "Only One is perfect. God." It is not given to us to be sinless, but we must and are perfectly able to be sincere, without guile, ulterior and harmful intentions and motives.

You are innately, intrinsically, good. You are God's children, Accept and acknowledge your royal and Divine inheritance! Dare to believe you are a child of the King of Kings. Walk the King's highway. All is yours!

To the man or woman who understands God as a loving parent, the same words are a source of comfort, solace, protection and support in our time of need. This open, receptive mind and heart welcome the higher understanding which knows, sees and is caring and concerned for our welfare, as is any true parent.

The open mind is willing, eager to accept God as all-good. How could that possibly be harmful? On the contrary, it becomes the joy and strength of life. The joy of the

Lord is your strength. Forgive yourself of any idea that you are wicked, in the sense of "bad," "evil," "sinful." If your intent is to better yourself without harming another, you are free, forgiven of wickedness.

Please do not be fearful or afraid of a word. Learn and think of what it conveys or means. We should be eager to learn, as children are eager and joyous to discover the world around them. As the mother watches over and protects her child, so is good God towards each of us. Psalm 139's fourth great truth reinforces this: *Thou has covered me in my mother's womb. I will praise thee, for I am fearfully and wonderfully made. Marvelous are they works and that my soul knoweth right well. You came out of the invisible and when the ovum was fertilized, it contained the archetype (pattern) of a man or a woman.*

Infinite intelligence created all of your organs, your body, from the Divine pattern embodied in the fertilized cell. Infinite intelligence knows all the processes and functions of your body and knows how to heal and restore any organ. Claim, feel, know and believe with all your mind, heart and soul. "The Infinite Healing Presence moves through every atom of my being, renewing and restoring to full and vitalizing, radiant health." Picture a river of golden light flowing through and within you—from the crown of your head to the soles of our feet.

If in the care of a physician, cooperate fully and remember to pray for his or her guidance and enlightenment. He or she is Divinely guided to do the right thing, right way, right time. Do not begrudge or resent the physician or remedy. They possess a wealth of healing knowledge and have your best interest at heart. Pray this way and both of our will be guided, directed, lead along the paths of ideal healing.

The psalmist wrote continuously about the leading and guidance of God. It is a practical and pragmatic characteristic of the Presence. Use same process of prayer to cure, correct, any and all phases of our being. You will discover health, wealth, congenial relationships, forming and taking shape in your experience.

Guidance is given in the form of inner promptings, urges, and ideas, and we quickly and soon learn to recognize we are being led along path and ways of contentment and perfect peace of mind. Meditate and contemplate Psalm 139, this Crown of all Psalms, and you discovered that guidance has already begun. Fear and worry will fade away and be replaced with confidence, optimism and strong, healthy, inspiring, spiritual thoughts, which will seep into your subconscious mind and restore you to a serene and happy life.

In a Nutshell

The four essential truths are these:

- First, we must accept God as a Presence who is omnipresent and universal.

- Second, omnipresence, God, being everywhere, is within us. We are in it. God is love; our relationship is as a beloved one.
- Third, the Presence is Omniscient: God knows all and sees all and being love, forgives Dare and have the heart or courage to believe and claim a loving, all-knowing God, which wants and desires you to know and receive far more than you know and desire to receive God.
- Fourth, the psalmist informs of a way to apply, use, these truths to heal, restore, and correct mind-body, conditions and relationships.

God is omnipresent. It is the very life of you. This Presence is always waiting for you to call up It. Regardless of the degree of bondage you may be in, this Presence and Power will respond as mercy, soothing, healing and restoring your soul.

The purpose and function of prayer, meditation, contemplation, is to cleanse the mind and to make the contents of the mind and heart obey our conscious direction. Literally, changing the habitual thought patterns and processes; make disciples of our mind and hearts.

You are innately, intrinsically, good. You are God's children. Accept and acknowledge your royal and Divine inheritance! Dare to believe you are a child of the King of Kings. Walk the King's highway. All is yours!

CHAPTER ELEVEN

Three Keys to Peace of Mind

I t is said that the kingdom of heaven is like a merchant, searching for fine pearls. When he has found a single pearl of great value, he goes and sells all of his possessions and buys it.

The pearl of great value and price is our awareness and perception that there is only one power and one cause in the midst of all phenomena—it is the holy one—the living presence of a living God.

The pearl of great value is our awareness and perception that all things (phenomenalistic evidences of life) come from one source. The ancients called it *the mind*, the mystics named it *the Divine*. We call it *life*. It is God within us, responding to thoughts of our mind, the meditations of our heart, our imaginings.

Metaphorically, classically, historically, pearls have been representative of valuable ideas, concepts and ideal which ennoble, inspire, elevate and lift up the minds and hearts of humankind (men and women, boys and girls) to the realization of the healing, creative power within.

It creates conditions, events, relationships, and circumstances of our daily lives in accordance to our dominant thoughts, ideations, and innermost feelings, according to their nature. The pearl is a simile for truth, which sets us free from deep-seated feelings and attitudes, which hold us, back.

Why the pearl? It isn't even classified as a jewel (such as emerald, sapphire, ruby, diamond), but a gem of far less value, monetarily. It is the product of an irritation, an abnormal growth within the shell of the mollusk: a living organism. It is the only gem (so far known) to appear as representative of life, living presence within.

It is when we become sufficiently "irritated," disturbed and troubled at the way we feel life is treating us that we truly seek and search for answers, and for a lasting sense of stability, security and quietude. So even in the midst of the troubled state, there is a hidden blessing, a benefit, to be found—if we have the eyes to see it and ears to hear it (both of which symbolize willingness and perception).

The thoughtful man or woman is dissatisfied with lesser quality pearls: passing or temporary happiness and joys. Are we not all seekers? Do we not always yearn for a fairer pearl? Money is good, but not without friendship. Friendship is good, but not outside a higher devotion, devotion to art and music is good, but not without a clear conscience; a clear conscience is good, but impossible without forgiveness. These are all good and very good and we should be thankful for them, and we should express our thanks to the healing presence within.

But our search is for that single pearl of greatest value, of surpassing worth in the words of the Bible, "The kingdom of heaven." What is heaven? What do these words mean to us? Scriptures are written in code and it is essential to decipher the code to find the very practical truths hidden or covered in scriptures, in the holy books of all religions.

Modern interpreters say that a state of consciousness in harmony with the presence, the thoughts of God, which are good (helpful, beneficial or beneficent). Heaven is everywhere. It is the orderly, lawful adjustment of God's kingdom in our own mind, body and affairs.

Heaven is within every one of us. A conscious attitude of mind, centered on the ideal state, the benefit that comes to mind when we exclaim, upon the realization of some good happening to ourselves or a loved one: "This is heaven on Earth!" "Heaven" equals the ideal and "Earth," its manifestation.

Obviously, the kingdom of God within is not material; it is spiritual. Heaven is the realm of pure ideas. Earth is the manifestation of these ideas.

A new consciousness creates new conditions, circumstances more in harmony with our higher ideas as we dwell upon them, mentally, emotionally, and spiritually.

We have to change within our thoughts, feelings, attitudes, and outlook about ourselves, other people and all things. We have to give up what we now hold (in consciousness) in exchange for that which we want. We cannot believe in the creative power within us while also holding the belief that other people and conditions are making or marring our lives.

Obviously, this is a contradiction and an impasse. Our parables tell us what we are to do, for we are like the merchant, seeking the one pearl of great value. We are to sell all our possessions and buy that one. A literal reading of this make no sense at all.

"Our possessions" are our preconceived ideas, opinions, and any conception of a God who shows favoritism. Our possessions include ill will, resentment, anger towards others, and towards ourselves for the mistakes we have made in the past.

This is a lesson in selection, discretion, choice and values. A sense of value is one of the most important developments in any person's life. Know the genuine from the counterfeit; the true from the false; the superior from the inferior; the valuable from the worthless.

It is not an accident that the person in the biblical story is a merchant, a businessman, apparently a successful one, as he possesses pearls to sell. The ability to judge values is most evident in the marketplace, for both buyer and seller, and the simplest mind in dealing with any commodity of the physical world can develop a keen sense of values.

The principle of selecting that, which is of value, is within us, rejecting that which is worthless, and we employ it every day. The principle of selecting the more valuable in preference to the less valuable extends upward, infinitely— as do all principles.

The kingdom of heaven is within, so we must learn to be good merchants within—our thoughts and feelings—to select with all the deliberate care and interest and involvement of one making an investment in the market. Select only those ideas that promote our well-being and prosperity and reject, refuse to accept, those which do not.

"Buy" one idea; "sell" it's opposite. We're always buying and selling. How often have you said, when hearing something that appeals to you, "I'll buy that?" This healthy, healing, wholesome process of value determination is the spiritual concept of forgiveness. It is an ongoing process of giving up and relinquishing the lesser for the greater, of renewing the mind and body with thoughts and words of truth.

It is through forgiveness that true spiritual healing is accomplished. Forgiveness removes the errors of the mind, and harmony results in every phase of our lives (the "body") in consonance with divine mind and divine principle, or law—dependable law. Errors of the mind, misunderstanding, are Biblical "sin"—failure to realize the creative, healing power of God is within.

The law is principle of truth; and truth is all that is good. There is no lasting, binding power in sin, or in error. If sin were real and enduring, like truth and goodness (in its highest sense) it could not be forgiven, neither could it be corrected nor replaced with a better, more valuable approach to life. You are spiritually being "healed," "made holy," wholesome, entire and complete.

Once enter into the forgiving attitude, a great light dawns in us, and we see what is meant when we read in the Bible "the son of man (ourselves) has authority to forgive sins." We forgive ourselves.

An inner change is essential, of necessity, for our own sakes in order to be at one with the healing presence. To forgive others, the past, with all its hurts and injustices, makes it possible to be forgiven.

Through the divine law of forgiveness, we cleanse, renew, our mind so we can be forgiven. Once we perceive and accept or "buy" the greatest of all truths, we are truly, sincerely and with effect, loving God.

Love is the pure essence of being that binds up our psychic wounds and heals and makes right anything and everything which may be wrong or in error in our lives.

In divine mind, love is the power that binds together in one magnificent harmony the universe. It is the harmonizing principle that sets us on the high road of the ancients to health, happiness, well-being, prosperity and peace of mind.

Divine love loves for the sake of loving. It that respect, it is impersonal just as the sun shines on the just and the unjust alike, it is offered to everyone. We are here to recognize and to personalize divine love. To remember that when we call to God for help, for guidance, we are really calling on divine love. It is the greatest unifying, most intelligent, all-knowing principle that we know.

It is divine love that brings our own to us; that adjusts misunderstandings; that restores, renews, and fulfills. Love therefore is fulfilling of the law. We, ourselves, fulfill the law of our life—once we sell all our possessions and purchase the one most valuable, the living presence within, as guide, counselor, healer, friend. The pearl of great price is our peace of mind in every condition.

Peace of mind is achieved by getting a very real sense of presence of God within you. The poet and mystic, Lord Alfred Tennyson wrote: "Speak to Him, for He hears; closer is He than breathing, nearer than hands and feet."

When we become quiet and still, we feel the divine response. A sense of quiet restfulness pervades and fills our mind and heart. It has been well said that peace is the power at the heart, the center, of God and ourselves. It is the pearl, glowing with a gorgeous, serene, translucent beauty all its own, permitting the passage of light in and through and all around us, even in the midst of darkness (the most difficult situation). It is our salvation; it is the solution to our problems.

Interesting that in times of emergency, the most difficult of situations, the ability, strength and power to cope is always there. It is divine love, supporting us, enabling us to manage, usually very well. Generally, it is the day-to-day pressures, tasks, demands, details, interruptions, and annoyances that overwhelm us.

We require, on occasion, something that helps us to turn and to return to our divine center. Why not purchase and mount a pearl? One of my most treasured presents is a small, stylized, modernistic, crystal shell. In it is embedded a single pearl.

A most favored art object because a gift from very dear friends and also serves as an inspiration. When nothing else brings calm, to see it shining, softly glowing in the sun, is a reminder of the presence—remember the pearl. It is a symbol of the kingdom of heaven, of God, presence, of peace, protection, provision, and happiness within, of all that we hold to be good and true in life.

This is real religion. It far transcends and surpasses theology. Jesus taught no theology. "Love God; forgive yourself and others." Love frees, forgives. It is the spirit of God. Jesus' admonition: "Sell all you have and follow me," then reveals a new dimension, and takes on a new meaning.

"Sell your possessions," means to forgive. Give up the lesser for the greater. "How much do I want what I think I want?" Enough to forgive so that I can experience and participate in life more fully "the life more abundant?" *Follow me* equals follow his instructions and example. You'll discover the meaning and purpose of your life and you will possess enduring peace of mind and lasting happiness.

Happiness usually is equated with recreation and some recreation is necessary to balanced life, but the really thoughtful individuals throughout history have suggested that happiness consists of creative action, and in fearlessly pursuing our own most noble instincts, ideals of our youth, thereby raising ourselves up from a life of struggling to do what is necessary for survival, to a life of doing what pleases the soul—"following the dictates of our heart."

Those who have demonstrated the courage to follow their start, to think independently, always seem to be somehow larger than life. Moses, Buddha, Plato, Jesus, Mohammed, Emerson, Einstein—philosophers, scientists, theologians. Dr. Albert Schweitzer was all three, and while most know him as the selfless physician who devoted his life to treating and healing the natives in the remote jungles of Africa, he was far more than that. In his book, *Legacy of Truth*, Dr. J. Kennedy Schultz wrote that Dr. Schweitzer has been described as "a renaissance man raised to spiritual dimensions," because of his wide-ranging expertise as a concert organist (and technician) and as an acknowledged authority on Johann Sebastian Bach. He received his first two doctorates in theology and one year later in philosophy. He was a professor as well as a highly respected biblical scholar.

When he decided that his real desire was to serve life and others in a really meaningful way, at the age of 30, he again became a student at the university where he was securely positioned for privileged, lifelong professorship—and entered into the study of medicine.

In his book *Out of My Life and Thought*, he referred to this period as "the most grueling seven years of my experience." Perhaps because he continued to give sermons every Sunday and organ recitals throughout Europe in order to fund his medical studies.

Only his incredible physical strength and an ironclad dynamic will allowed him to survive and to succeed so brilliantly. In 1965, at the age of 90, he passed on, still in full possession of his faculties and his enormous energies permitted him to treat his beloved patients.

With the enormous capability of this practical mystic, and his exceptional education, the entire world respected, admired and assisted in bringing to him all that was needed to supply his hospital in what is now Gabon in Africa.

Three ideas formed the philosophy of Dr. Schweitzer. Even though he was a theologian first, his desire was to impart some truth that would include all people, whether or not they were religiously inclined.

A sense of the mystery and awe—"a great mystery of the Eternal for all men and women in every walk of life."

With all our technology, we can't create an insect. "I want to meet a man, as a man, on his own terms" not to change or convert him, but to respect him just as he is.

Everyone needs a purpose in order to realize God-given and infinite potential, be it humble or very great. And a dedication to those purposes, so that we become completely involved in them. Everyone can contribute to life to a certain degree. To replenish or replace the gifts that have been offered us. Become interested in others and their welfare: We rise to heights of which we may not have been aware.

His total philosophy, which makes the others possible, is deceptively simple, but all encompassing. This he termed, "A reverence for life." He gave us a legacy of three great ideas, "keys" which unlock the gates of our minds and hearts:

The very mystery that life—the God-mind—exists in us, the world, and the universe.

Our purpose is realized in serving life, not merely to be served.

A reverence for life.

A complete sense of commitment and we enter into a more comprehensive life and we fulfill our purpose in being here. "Sell" all our less inspiring "possessions" and "purchase" the one great sense of reverence for life and the peace that passes understanding and becomes and remains on, forever—the kingdom of heaven on Earth.

Worry and fear can only dominate your life if you let it. You have the power to eliminate them from your life. You have the Presence within you, the strength to change your life. By prayer and meditation, by commitment to your spiritual self, by trust in the Divine, you will overcome your fears and concerns. By feeding positive thoughts into your conscious mind, your subconscious mind will respond positively when faced with problems and find solutions that will result in a happier, more peaceful and more rewarding life.

In a Nutshell

Are we not all seekers? Money is good, but not without friendship. Friendship is good, but not outside a higher devotion, devotion to art and music is good, but not without a clear conscience; a clear conscience is good, but impossible without forgiveness. These are all good and very good and we should be thankful for them, and we should express our thanks to the healing presence within.

The kingdom of heaven is within, so we must learn to be good merchants within—our thoughts and feelings. To select with all the deliberate care and interest and involvement of one making an investment in the market. Select only those ideas that promote our well-being and prosperity and reject, refuse to accept, those which do not.

Love is the power that binds together in one magnificent harmony the universe. It is the harmonizing principle that sets us on the high road of the ancients to health, happiness, well-being, prosperity and peace of mind.

Remember and apply Dr. Albert Schweizer's philosophy, which he termed, "A reverence for life." He gave us a legacy of three great ideas, "keys" which unlock the gates of our minds and hearts:

1. The very mystery that life—the God-mind—exists in us, the world, the universe.

2. Our purpose is realized in serving life, not merely to be served.

3. A reverence for life.

ABOUT THE AUTHOR

A native of Ireland who resettled in America, Joseph Murphy, Ph.D., D.D. (1898–1981) was a prolific and widely admired New Thought minister and writer, best known for his metaphysical classic, *The Power of Your Subconscious Mind*, an international bestseller since it first appeared on the self-help scene in 1963. A popular speaker, Murphy lectured on both American coasts and in Europe, Asia, and South Africa. His many books and pamphlets on the auto-suggestive and metaphysical faculties of the human mind have entered multiple editions—some of the most poignant of which appear in this volume. Murphy is considered one of the pioneering voices of affirmative-thinking philosophy.